ONLY WONDER COMPREHENDS

4. A contemporary priest's "care of souls" in response to such issues as disbelief, pacifism, same-sex marriage, and women priests.
5. A coda to recap and illustrate John's love of life and the vitality of his faith.

As noted, John Garvey was steeped in the Christian tradition, in particular the theology, practice, and luminous heritage of the Orthodox communion. Yet he remained ever attentive to the promptings of the Holy Spirit wherever they might be discovered—and wherever they led him. It is hoped that this brief selection of his writings from *Commonweal* will inspire readers to cultivate a similar sense of attentiveness and commitment, for as the author himself observed: "Religious traditions are meant to transform us, not to affirm us as we are."

It was my privilege—as an editor at *Commonweal*— to work with John Garvey over many years, and to share ideas, suggestions, and much laughter. I am indebted to his wife Regina for her encouragement and continuing inspiration; and to *Commonweal*'s editor, Paul Baumann, and its publisher, Thomas Baker, for their direction and support in this project. The same must be said of the entire staff, but in particular Ellen Koneck, special-projects director, and a number of willing and unsung interns, among them Caroline Belden, Nick Haggerty, and Catherine Larrabee, who gathered, read, and assembled megareams of material. I hope and trust that readers will enjoy the fruit of their handiwork as much as I. Read on!

Patrick Jordan

GROUNDINGS

Climbing Trees

I grew up at the edge of Springfield, Illinois, across the street from open spaces, an active farm with cattle and corn growing in a field that adjoined the pasture. Beyond the farm was a forest, and another forest lay a few houses away from the north side of our house. After a few years the farm died but the fields remained, and the fields and forests were great places to explore and play in. I loved one tree in particular; its branches grew in a way that made it perfect for climbing. When I was nine or ten I would climb it nearly to the top, which was as high as the roofline of our house, and when storms were coming and the wind picked up, I liked getting as close to the top as I could, holding on when the tree began lashing back and forth. I was able to get away with this because my parents had lots of other, younger kids to herd and were often distracted.

Though I didn't really appreciate it at the time, the tree was my introduction to philosophy and a sense of deep mystery, of something sacred. I loved reading about science and had recently learned that we can only see part of the full spectrum of light. Looking at the tree one day I realized that I really couldn't see all of it; there were colors poured out there that were beyond my vision. Then I realized that I could see the

tree from only one angle, that of a small boy. If I moved a few
feet the branches took on a different configuration. If I were
a giant, seeing it from above, it would seem very different. (It
was easy to imagine this because one of the ways I found it
tolerable to eat broccoli was to pretend I was a giant eating
trees.) If I saw it from the perspective of a grasshopper it would
be unimaginably vast. I slowly came to understand that I could
see the tree from only one point of view at a time, always in a
limited way.

Still, what was the tree apart from my ways of seeing it? It
plainly was something that would in some ways always be
beyond me, mysterious, largely unknowable—no matter how
many things I could know about it. Only God could really
know the tree as it was; only God could know the final *thatness*
of the tree. Years later I found the same sense of the deep silence and mystery of things in Rilke's poetry, with its sense
that this silence speaks to us, and must, and that something
human dies when we fail to listen.

I have been very aware of this in recent months, because
after years in a busy parish ministry I am now attached to a
church where the pastor does virtually all the work, and I have
a lot of time to write and read and be alone. I do occasionally
have to fill in for the pastor, or substitute for priests in other
parishes, but for the most part my days are filled with solitude.
I have found that I like and even need this; and I know it's a
rare luxury. In a way, it is a return for me to the day when I
first saw the tree as full of mystery.

To a certain extent it is also a necessity, for at least some of
our day, to spend time alone and in silence. A certain amount
of silence and solitude is necessary for any appreciation of the
sacred. There are times in life when this is nearly impossible
. . . for example, when you are a young parent. My fear,
though, is not that some people find this impossible; the prob-

lem is rather that most of us flee from it. I know that even when I am alone, I like music in the background, or the sound of the radio. I have to force myself to turn it off and simply sit down. But it is only when we go against the grain and force ourselves to do this that we begin to see the usual noise our minds make, that we begin to let that clatter settle down and to sense the real world around us. This is necessary for any serious prayer or meditation. Otherwise the words of prayer are not listened to in any depth, and the silence that is necessary as the place into which the words are spoken will not be real for us.

It is less and less possible to do this. No, it is almost always possible to do this, but we live in an age when the temptations not to experience solitude in any way are all around us. I often get up very early, and I am amazed when I look outside our apartment and see someone walking down the street at 5:30 in the morning with a cell phone to the side of his head, talking away. The sight of all those people chattering on cell phones all the time is the clearest recent sign of how terrified we are to be alone.

Once I was away from television for a few years; then I was sent to a convention, turned on the television set in the hotel room, and was astounded at the visual racket. It didn't take long to get acclimated all over again, but the time I had spent away from that particular form of distraction made me aware of how noisy, lurid, and even violent its effects can be.

The problem is not only that it is good for us to live with a sense of mystery and the sacred, or that we are deprived of something good when we do not. The effects of this constant noise and distraction are deeper and even more ominous. It is not as if the sacred were a luxury we can turn to if we are so inclined, an optional good thing. Rather, a sense of the sacred is necessary if we are to become truly human, and we are twisted away from what we are meant to be when we ignore the sacred. Although too much emphasis can be put on felt experience, where prayer and the Christian life are concerned, we must have an experience of the sacred to really be able to believe in it, and it can't be experienced without the kind of prayer that can be born only in silence.

February 24, 2006

Confidence v. Certainty

At the end of *The Wizard of Oz* (still wonderful after all these years), the Wicked Witch of the West is confounded, a failure. Dissolving in a puddle of water, she moans, "What a world, what a world." I'm with her.

Many religious people feel a need for clarity. They need to have a sense that they are right, or at least on the right path and relatively sure of their direction. This is an understandable yearning, but what may be insufficiently appreciated is the important place for confusion and uncertainty in our spiritual life.

What we cannot possibly know or understand with certainty occupies much more of the universe than what we do know, and our uncertainties may be a more important part of who we ultimately will be. I think of the depth of what the Incarnation must mean for all created life, for all matter, and realize that the dogma as we know it, profound and deep as it is, is only the surface. What cannot possibly be put into words matters more than what can be.

The desire to be absolutely clear about the best doctrinal or moral path is understandable but probably misguided. I remember a time when as a young man I went to confession, trying to make sense of a moral dilemma that was a knotted mess. The old priest listening to me said, "Just confess it as it is before God." No doubt this saved him some time, but it was also liberating. I saw that God obviously knows what I cannot know about myself, can fathom it and deal with it and heal it, and I can do none of this. But even putting it this way anthropomorphizes God. It doesn't account for the constant mystery of God's presence.

When I was younger I expected certain forms of guidance and moral direction from prayer, but I have come to think that we never get these things except in ways that are potentially misleading. Instead of clear direction, we may be blessed in prayer with a sense of presence and mystery, which tells us nothing.

As Christians, we tend to make too much of morality. On the right there is an emphasis on "family values" and sexual morality, and on the left social justice, but Jesus has little to say about specific forms of moral behavior. Here a certain case can be made for those who speak of being "spiritual but not religious." This designation may often indicate a shallow understanding, but it may also be a natural reaction to the moralism of people for whom being religious means having strong opinions about everything from same-sex marriage to gun control (on either side of those issues). The spiritual but not religious may find themselves more moved by the experience of beauty or feelings of gratitude than by the things openly religious people point to as important, and they are not wrong to feel alienated from what is often presented as Christianity.

Jesus does not challenge us to be good; he says, "You are to be perfect, as your heavenly Father is perfect." True compassion comes not from decent behavior, important as that is, but from insight born of gratitude and surrender. It requires a thorough transformation. We start out on that path to the Kingdom by becoming "like little children." And here we have to take care not to fall into a sentimental trap. Our current notions of childhood are only as old as the Victorians and come clouded with visions of innocence and purity. The English Dominican Simon Tugwell has pointed out a more ancient meaning: Little children don't know anything. When we understand this about ourselves we are ready to begin.

Our true understanding of the following of Christ comes when we are willing to place ourselves in the hands of the living God, not knowing anything that has not been shown to us in Christ, not knowing where we may be led, but having confidence that whatever God has in store for us will involve the depth of the love we see in Jesus' Cross and Resurrection. Confidence isn't the same thing as certainty. It matters more. It opens a door that certainty closes, and it allows us to hope.

June 1, 2013

A Tree Full of Monkeys

*I*n the earliest years of Christian teaching, dogma was proclaimed only when a denial of something (Jesus' humanity or his divinity, for example) made it necessary. The articulated doctrine of the Trinity emerged slowly, from the more important domain of silence into the lesser domain of words. Words, even at their best, are inadequate and prone to misunderstanding, leading to concepts and imaginary constructs that can get in the way of participation in the mystery.

We need words, but we need them to take us to the place where we realize their inadequacy. They point us in the right direction, but they are never sufficient.

In dealing with other religions—or for that matter with serious agnosticism—we should at once maintain fidelity to our deepest belief while realizing that our belief cannot exhaust or fully describe the mystery we are trying to point to. I believe that the fullness of what can be found in Christ shows us the relationship between creation and God in a way nothing else can. But as we sit together before the silence at the depth of everything made, I cannot say that a Buddhist or Jew or agnostic might not also be able to tell me something he or she has found there, something I need to hear and might never have been able to discover on my own.

Even in its inadequacy, however, language is an indicator of the reality of the spiritual. Language points to a world beyond the merely material and quantifiable. To have a word for something is a kind of miracle.

In "God's Grandeur," Gerard Manley Hopkins speaks of the things that get between us and a clearer sense of our true condition:

> And all is seared with trade; bleared, smeared with toil;
> And wears man's smudge and shares man's smell: the soil
> Is bare now, nor can foot feel, being shod.

When I read the poem I think of Moses being told to take off his sandals because he stands on holy ground, the point being: let nothing get between you and *this*, *this* being a crucial moment, a place, even the feeling at the soles of your feet.

This is a good argument for contemplative and meditative practice, seen not as something reserved for monks, nuns, and other people who are expected to pray seriously and meditate, but for all of us. It takes an effort to be clear about the moment we are in. It requires taking time—time a lot of people claim they don't have; but they can surf the Web, read the Styles section of the *New York Times*, watch *CSI: Des Moines* (is that on yet?), etc. We need, through practice, to be made aware of what is wrong about ordinary waking consciousness, and it takes an effort to learn this.

Ordinary waking consciousness swarms, pops, bubbles up with reactions, opinions, lines of thought, and is generally swept along in this stream. It interests me that every serious religious practice encourages us to resist this swarming, while nearly all our current practices (Twitter, Facebook, texting, etc.) encourage nearly constant distraction. I think of Ramakrishna's metaphor for the way the mind is: a tree full of monkeys jumping from branch to branch. Or I think of the fathers and mothers of the desert. They compare the way our minds ordinarily work to a hive swarming with bees, or a small pool of stirred-up muddy water that needs time to settle. It says something strange about our culture that even the value of stillness now needs to be explained.

Most churches, most places of worship, ignore this. Morality and "our teaching" (whatever that may be) are pushed, at the expense of how we absorb, or fail to absorb, anything at all. Our understandable inclination to follow ideas and currents of thought that appeal to us is something almost no religious community is willing to contend with seriously; but it matters, especially at a time when distraction and ideological reinforcement matter more to the culture than sober clarity does. This inattention disrupts our lives at every level, religious, political, and aesthetic. Serious prayer, in the form of prayer of the heart (the repetition of the name of Jesus, in one of several forms, done with attention over a period of time) or serious meditation (sitting still, quietly, *not* following the scramble), or simply spending lots of time in silence can reveal this—can begin to make us feel what's directly underfoot. Prayer, meditation, and silence can begin to help us understand where we really are, in the presence of the sacred, before the burning bush, before a God who says "I will be what I will be." It's a beginning.

July 16, 2010

Admitting Ignorance

Believers are often challenged with this question: How can you believe that God cares more for human beings than for other creatures, or any other part of creation? We have answered too confidently sometimes, almost as if we could know the mind of God. We know that God does love human beings, and the Cross and Resurrection show the extent and depth of that love.

But we do not know that God does not love the rest of creation in ways we cannot fathom. I remember a poem by Jorge Luis Borges in which the Word becomes flesh for every part of creation—a tiger for the sake of tigers, and so forth. While the particular Christian metaphor may not be relevant to the rest of creation—and Borges was himself apparently agnostic—this does point us toward a necessary humility. It is impossible for us to imagine how God delights in the Horsehead Nebula or in sea anemones, but it is also impossible to imagine that he does not.

Look at the delight in creation that shines in Psalm 104, which is crowded with trees, animals, people bringing forth wine and bread from God's earth, and the "[y]oung lions roar for prey; / they seek their food from God." And these wonderful lines:

> How varied are your works, LORD!
>> In wisdom you have made them all;
>> the earth is full of your creatures.
> There is the sea, great and wide!
>> It teems with countless beings,
>> living things both large and small.
> There ships ply their course
>> and Leviathan, whom you formed to play with.

It is a delight that the last line can be translated, "Leviathan, whom you made to play with." This reminds me of Brueghel's *Landscape with the Fall of Icarus,* a panorama of human activity, with a man plowing, a ship getting set to sail, and, in one corner, two tiny legs going into the water. Both the painting and the psalm are antidotes to human self-importance, even as they celebrate something deeply human.

The universe is a spiritual reality that manifests itself materially. Matter is not its foundation. This cannot be proven, but it can be discerned in partial ways, through prayer and meditation, even liturgically.

By "spiritual" I do not mean something ethereal or specter-like; I mean something more real than what can be weighed and measured. It can be encountered. It is interesting that the most fruitful Buddhist/Christian meetings have been among contemplative monks, who spend a lot of time in stillness.

Rather than use a word like "spiritual," which has been worked to death in many unhelpful ways, it might be better to say that the universe is the expression of something more than matter and energy.

And it is important not to impose our metaphors—legal, architectural, dramatic—on what this means, by lurching into talk of a divine plan or intention. The "thatness" of the universe is its mystery, as Wittgenstein saw. And it really is beyond words, or the sort of analysis science brings to understanding.

The problem with much atheistic writing is that it confuses extremely close description, the best currently available to us (this is science's province and genius), with real explanation. The problem with too many religious writers is that they try to explain too much. We really must be able to say, even at times when an answer may seem crucial, "I don't know." Here the Orthodox idea of the *theologoumenon* is important. You can say, "It might be like this—you may believe it, and it won't contradict what has been revealed—but it may not be like this." Truth is approached humbly, and the approach is a form of seeking rather than an insistence on certainty at every point. There are some things that are essential to Christianity: the completely divine and completely human nature of Jesus, the belief that he shows us what the Father is like, his death for us and his Resurrection for us, his command that we love one another, even our enemies.

After that we are left to see, in a tradition that includes the lives of many holy and perceptive men and women, how these beliefs are worked out, and what we may learn by sitting every day in prayer, and joining with others in the Eucharist, as we wait for God's will to be revealed—usually, though not always, in silence.

June 15, 2007

Telling the Christian Story

The idea that the universe is ultimately without meaning—an idea advanced by many of the new atheists—has often struck me, and other believers, as nihilistic and even antihuman. I've heard atheist scientists rhapsodize about the feeling of awe, even reverence, they feel in the presence of the beauty everywhere and at every level of the cosmos; but its beauty is something only *we* can see and feel, and promises nothing. If beauty and such experiences as love and deep joy ultimately mean nothing and have nothing to do with the being of the universe itself, it seems a profound cheat.

Recently, however, I heard a radio interview with a naturalist who spoke with great joy about the evolution of flightless birds, and I began to understand more sympathetically how an atheist or agnostic might delight in the varied and wonderful things that surround us, and still feel that even if the universe ultimately has nothing to do with what we value, what we value is nevertheless precious. As a Christian, I believe that love and beauty have to do with the meaning of matter and energy and all that exists—but finally this is an act of faith.

Such an act of faith probably comes more easily if you grow up surrounded by a culture that reinforces the belief in a meaning that goes deep down into the heart of existence, and if it is presented in a sympathetic way and manifested in admirable lives. My own perceptions of the way things finally are were formed in the context of a family and church and stories, many of them stories of saints, and not a few myths (especially Norse ones), all of them pointing, though not always clearly, in a direction that made sense: We are here for a reason, and we are meant to learn what it is, and live it out honorably. I saw it in the lives of some saints, and also the lives of people who were not necessarily religious but were noble and brave and compassionate. King Arthur mattered a lot more to me than St. Jerome.

The point is that this sort of shared overarching culture once influenced the way we look at life to a much greater degree than it does now and (more to the point) ever will again. There is now no prevailing mythos, no Christendom or Byzantium or Holy Roman Empire, no felt necessity to accept in any way a surrounding story that gives meaning to life. Once you move away from parental authority there is no social or moral pressure to accept such an overarching point of view. These "surrounds" did provide a sense of identity and meaning for the majority (Grimm's fairy tales show the dark side of this, for Jews in particular); and in countries that still insist on ethnic and religious identity as a sign of belonging, it continues in an attenuated way. But our distracted, media-saturated environment and loss of any serious common culture or collective memory means that even in traditional societies the surrounds operate less effectively, and people experience a sense of choice about belief, whether the belief has to do with faith, politics, ethics, or aesthetics.

The experience of choice has expanded, and some would claim its freedom as a morally good thing. I don't think so: I think it's morally neutral, depending on the choice. But I reflect on the fact that my own decision to become an Orthodox

Christian was clarified when I realized I was remaining Roman Catholic only because of what other people thought and expected, when I believed what the Orthodox Church believes and felt I had no moral alternative. In another time, another culture, could I have made this decision? Maybe, at certain points during the Reformation period, or when princes were changing their own religious allegiances for reasons of state and whole regions moved with them—but those were communal moves, and I was making my decision in a solely personal way. This is in some ways a postmodern phenomenon. Many more Americans than ever before have shifted from the confession of their birth to another, or to none at all.

All of which is to say that the church of the future must understand that the *status quo ante* can't be restored. *Pace* Pope Benedict, Christian Europe is gone forever, and *pace* Patriarch Bartholomew, no one cares about Constantinople's jurisdiction over the Barbarian lands and the diaspora. These are dead categories. We are on new ground, with no recourse to any common surrounding story; nor, given the scandals in all our churches, to any institutional moral authority. The argument now must be humble and persuasive, and the message must be the basic story itself. Does the church remember what that is? Can it tell the story as a matter of life and death, and make it mean something to people who have no reason to believe that bishops or priests have anything to offer? The positive and moving reception given to movies like *Of Gods and Men* and *Into Great Silence* might offer a clue about how to get people to pay attention to what Christianity can mean in particular lives. It's a hopeful beginning.

May 6, 2011

The New Atheists

Reports of Mother Teresa's long dark night made more news than they should have, I thought. Then I had second thoughts: this might lead to a serious discussion of faith and certainty, which are not at all the same thing. There were a few thoughtful letters to the editor, and Christopher Hitchens's tin-eared *Newsweek* review, and not much more. But certain themes kept cropping up, and they matter in the debate between serious believers and serious nonbelievers. I stress the word "serious" here because the more public debates about belief (the ones involving the religious beliefs of politicians, creationism vs. evolution, etc.) are not serious at all. But the debate about faith and certainty does matter, and the stakes are high because there are important moral visions at both ends of the argument.

According to the new atheists, what cannot be demonstrated scientifically should be believed only in the most tentative way. They go further than this: faith means absolute certainty, they say, and is false because, unlike the scientific method, it doesn't offer the possibility of proof or falsifiability. Mother Teresa's experience of God's absence, her doubts, are seen as signs of a lack of faith.

This idea of faith as certainty without provability has nothing to do with the experience of most of the believers I know.

Certainty isn't the point. It may be for some fundamentalists, but they aren't the people you find in most churches or synagogues. For most of the faithful, what is interesting about the new atheism is what it does not find valuable.

When you reduce everything to a materialistic level—when you say that what can really be believed is only that which can be weighed, tested, replicated, or falsified—you marginalize everything that is of most value to most people. You say, in effect, that love, honor, nobility, beauty, generosity, or anything wonderful or virtuous, are epiphenomena; those things we value most are possibly illusory readings of essentially material events. They are all subjective reactions, and have no grounding in material reality, which has, finally, no meaning, no essential goodness. Goodness itself is something with no objective reality.

Mother Teresa lived in a larger universe, as did Thérèse of Lisieux, who had a similar experience of God's absence toward the end of her life; also the doubting father who wanted Jesus to cure his son: "I believe; help my unbelief." What they place their faith in is not certainty, but rather the belief that the universe is grounded in meaning, and this meaning is to be found not in proofs but in the most profound movements of the heart.

The problem believers have with the new atheists comes down to this: What atheists see as epiphenomenal is all that matters to most of us. The love that we feel, the joy, the delight in natural beauty, the ways we are moved by acts of compassion, heroism, and generosity—all of these are, we believe, essential to the way the universe is. The glory we find in looking at the Horsehead Nebula is not our subjective reaction to a meaningless phenomenon; the glory is part of a dialogue between us and God. We are meant to find it beautiful, and this is part of our own meaning.

But there is a moral element in the new atheism that believers can miss. It is a protest against the cruelty of a universe in which believers can insist that a good God is in charge, when children can be terribly abused, or can be swept away in tsunamis. This is not an unreasonable response to the smugness of some comfortable forms of religious belief—the sort that can say, when war has claimed the life of your next-door neighbor's son and yours has returned home safely, "God was with us." Well, yes—and not with your neighbor? There is something wrong with forms of belief that are so sentimental and complacent, and anyone, believer or nonbeliever, is right to find them shallow.

Pope Benedict's encyclical *Spe salvi* rightly emphasizes the connection between hope and faith, and also acknowledges the moral element in nonbelief. I think he is right in his analysis of the ultimate end of nonbelief: it is finally a form of nihilism and hopelessness. Although the encyclical does have a number of moments when the pope's academic background is all too apparent, it is very much worth reading. I hope Orthodox and Protestants understand that this is not some internal Catholic message, but a word that challenges all believers, and all nonbelievers. Without a universe grounded in meaning, and meaning understood as finally compassionate, nothing can be celebrated, and nothing can be condemned, in any honest or serious way. What atheists of the new variety see as epiphenomenal is the ground of what most human beings have celebrated from the beginning of human history, even before they knew the joy of the gospel.

January 18, 2008

PORTALS

The Fiction of Philip K. Dick

*P*hilip K. Dick (1928–82) was the kind of science-fiction writer who is read and praised by people who don't like science fiction. His fame moved beyond the genre's ghetto after some of his novels and short stories were turned into movies—*Blade Runner* (1982), *Minority Report* (2002), and *A Scanner Darkly* (2006), to name a few. He is sometimes compared to Jorge Luis Borges, one of the finest short-story writers, and his work has influenced many authors (genre-bending Jonathan Lethem, for example) and filmmakers (the Wachowski brothers, directors of *The Matrix*).

Just as critics dub certain writers' visions of the world "Orwellian" or "Kafkaesque," some now use the awkward term "Dickian." Dick's paranoid vision is a unique, sad, funny, and—in its strange and sometimes very moving manner—even ennobling way to think about what we are meant to be as humans. In his later work, Dick's outlook became deeply, even explicitly, informed by a Gnostic sense of the struggle to be fully human. Ancient Gnosticism was, among other things, concerned with the dilemma of humanity trapped in delusion, imprisoned in a world ruled by malign and unseen forces—a recurrent theme in Dick's work.

What does science fiction have to say about human nature? For many serious readers, this is Geek City, a corner of genre fiction inhabited by sad and lonely people who go to Star Trek conventions and collect action figures. The science-fiction writer Theodore Sturgeon is credited with what has entered the wider critical discourse as "Sturgeon's Law." When it was said of science fiction that "90 percent of it is crap," his answer was, "90 percent of everything is crap." Who can disagree? Serious science-fiction criticism finds examples of imagined alternatives that illuminate our own world in Plato's description of Atlantis in the *Timaeus*, in his vision of an ideal society in *The Republic*, and in Thomas More's imaginary society in *Utopia*. Some writers prefer another name for the genre, "speculative fiction," since much science fiction has little to do with science. Whatever term you choose, the best examples show that one way to see our situation clearly is to imagine another, very different one. This can be done by placing a story in the remote past, an alternative present, or a near or far future. Philip K. Dick was the writer who did it best.

The animating idea behind Dick's fiction—hardly original in itself—is that things are not as they seem. This is, of course, a major part of any religious insight—and as an Episcopalian, Dick understood this. Walker Percy's essay "The Message in the Bottle," for example, describes an island (this could be the beginning of a sci-fi plot) where everything is pleasant. Life seems good for all its inhabitants; then someone walking along a beach finds a bottle with the message, "Don't despair, help is on the way." This is what the Christian gospel says to a complacent, obtuse world, and it is not unlike one of Dick's plots. In many of his stories, as in Gnostic theology, the world is depicted as not merely asleep, but deliberately deceived. Any remedy or salvation will therefore have to include a battle against powers that not only seem insane, but are evil. Overcoming the ruse requires special insight or special revelation that is shared by only a few.

This theme of widespread deception is woven throughout several of Dick's plots. In *The Simulacra* (1964), the U.S. president is an android, but the citizenry has no idea. In *The Penultimate Truth* (1964), World War III starts with a fight between two superpowers. The battle begins on Mars, spreads to Earth, and is fought by robots. Humans are forced to live and work underground in huge shelters. The war ends, but the people are told that the battle rages above them on an uninhabitable surface. Meanwhile, the authorities continue to generate false war stories while they themselves live a bucolic life on the earth above. In *The Zap Gun* (1967), two great superpowers are at peace, and citizens of both nations are reassured that they are secure because of their side's superior arsenal—but the weapons are designed not to function. Weapon design is, in effect, a kind of conceptual art, although the fact that the weapons do not work is kept from the masses. This is what keeps the world truly disarmed. When aliens threaten the earth, the weapon designers have to come up with something that really functions. There is an implicit Gnosticism here: only a select few know what is going on; most of humanity is sleepwalking.

This isn't a happy point of view, to be sure. Yet what's missing from the film adaptations of Dick's work (of which the best are *Minority Report* and the director's cut of *Blade Runner*) is Dick's humor. Even his darkest stories are laced with funny moments. Another quality missing in the movies is Dick's enduring compassion for the sadness of ordinary, confused human existence. His stories usually take place in a future, or in an alternate reality, where paranoia reigns, where appearances cannot be trusted, where people may be androids—robots made to resemble humans—and androids may be whatever human beings are, where the world we are presented with is a lie.

Dick's life was messy. (Lawrence Sutin has written a good biography, *Divine Invasions: A Life of Philip K. Dick*, Carroll

& Graf, 2005.) He was born in Chicago in 1928 and died in 1982; his twin sister died in infancy. Dick's parents moved to California and divorced. He lived with his mother until he matriculated at UC Berkeley for a short time, majoring in German. He was fascinated by German culture. After dropping out of college, he worked in a record store, and music plays an important part in much of his work. He was married and divorced five times, used drugs, was convinced at various points that the FBI was after him, feared for his sanity, and hoped for spiritual deliverance.

At the same time, Dick felt a keen loyalty to many friends, whose lives were often as complicated as his own. His novels are full of regular people with ordinary, often dull jobs; they struggle for decency, sometimes fail, sometimes succeed. There is always something sad, frustrating, and funny about their struggles, and I can't think of another science-fiction writer who comes close to describing this sort of ordinary life with such compassion. The science-fiction novelist Ursula K. Le Guin once wrote that Dick's characters reminded her of Dickens's; sometimes you remember one and can't place which novel he or she appears in, but the humanity remains vivid. Dick drew from his own life, sometimes quite directly, in writing his novels. *A Scanner Darkly* is about drug use—based in large part on his own experience—and it's scary. It begins, "Once a guy stood all day shaking bugs from his hair." It contains the only funny suicide scene I've ever read, and at the end of the novel Dick uncharacteristically explains what he has just written:

> This is a novel about some people who were punished entirely too much for what they did. They wanted to have a good time, but they were like children playing in the street; they could see one after another of them being killed—run over, maimed, destroyed—but they continued to play any-

how. . . . Drug misuse is not a disease, it is a decision, like the decision to step out in front of a moving car. You would call that not a disease but an error in judgment. When a bunch of people begin to do it, it is a social error, a lifestyle. In this particular lifestyle the motto is "Be happy now because tomorrow you are dying," but the dying begins almost at once, and the happiness is a memory. It is, then, only a speeding up, an intensifying, of the ordinary human existence. It is not different from your lifestyle, it is only faster.

Before movies made him known beyond science-fiction circles, Dick's best-known work was *The Man in the High Castle*. It won the Hugo award (science fiction's highest) in 1962. It describes an alternative 1962 America, in which the Nazis and the Japanese won World War II. There are some nicely imagined touches (Americans forge Wild West artifacts to sell to wealthy Japanese collectors; Germans fly rapidly around the world not in jets, but in passenger rockets), but at the center of the novel is a search for the author of *The Grasshopper Lies Heavy*, an alternative-world tale in which Germany and Japan were defeated. This alternative world is not the one we know, the one that really followed from the defeat of Hitler; and finally, it is suggested that the world the protagonists live in isn't real either. The *I Ching*, an ancient Chinese text, figures in the book's plot, and Dick apparently used its chance-based methods of divination in composing the story. Although Dick never alluded to it, this sense of not being able to know what reality really is reminded me of the Taoist sage Chuang Tsu's dream that he was a butterfly: it wasn't clear to him whether he was Chuang Tsu dreaming that he was a butterfly, or a butterfly dreaming that he was Chuang Tsu.

In 1978, Dick delivered a lecture, "How to Build a Universe That Doesn't Fall Apart Two Days Later." In it, he said: "The two basic topics that fascinate me are 'What is reality?' and

'What constitutes the authentic human being?'" This fascination went back to his first published story, "Roog," which "had to do with a dog who imagined that the garbage men who came every Friday morning were stealing valuable food that the family had carefully stored away in a safe metal container. Every day, members of the family carried out paper sacks of nice ripe food, stuffed them into the metal container, shut the lid tightly—and when the container was full, these dreadful-looking creatures came and stole everything but the can . . . [T]he dog's extrapolation was in a sense logical, given the facts at his disposal."

Dick's approach was not always so light. In an angry short story about abortion, "The Pre-Persons," he wrote of a future in which the courts had decided that a person was a real human being only when capable of doing algebra. Children not yet old enough to grasp algebraic concepts lived in dread of extermination trucks that could come and take them away. Dick's antiabortion stance led the feminist science-fiction writer Joanna Russ to send Dick a letter, "the nastiest letter I've ever received." Although he later apologized for any hurt feelings, he said, "for the pre-persons' sake, I am not sorry."

If Dick's early work sometimes had an implicitly Gnostic aspect, that quality became more explicit in his later writing. In 1974, Dick, recovering from minor surgery, answered his door for a delivery of painkillers. The young woman delivering the medication was wearing a fish pendant, and when he asked what it was, she told him that it was a sign worn by the early Christians. In "How to Build a Universe," he writes,

> I suddenly experienced what I later learned is called *an-amnesis*—a Greek word meaning, literally, "loss of forget-fulness." I remembered who I was and where I was. In an instant, in the twinkling of an eye, it all came back to me.

And not only could I remember it but I could see it. The girl was a secret Christian and so was I. We lived in fear of detection by the Romans. We had to communicate with secret signs. She had just told me all this, and it was true.

For a short time, as hard as this is to believe or explain, I saw fading into view the black, prison-like contours of hateful Rome. But, of much more importance, I remembered Jesus, who had just recently been with us, and had gone temporarily away, and would very soon return. My emotion was one of joy. We were secretly preparing to welcome him back. It would not be long. And the Romans did not know. They thought he was dead, forever dead. That was our great secret, our joyous knowledge. Despite all appearances, Christ was going to return, and our delight and anticipation was boundless.

Dick was never entirely clear about what that experience meant. But he was convinced that something of great significance had happened to him, and wrote at length about his encounters with what he called "the cosmic Christ" in a free-form journal called "The Exegesis," in which he understood Christ as part of a continuity which included Ikhnaton, Zoroaster, and Hephaestus. This syncretism is typical of Gnosticism. Dick's efforts to explain what all this meant are less interesting than the work that came from the experience, his final three novels.

Dick's visions and dreams coalesced in the *VALIS* trilogy— VALIS being an acronym for Vast Active Living Intelligence System, or God (of a sort). The most tangled, complicated, and autobiographical is the first, *VALIS* (1981). It is the least successful of the three, but worth reading because of its seriousness and its painful closeness to Dick's own life. The plot of *VALIS* contains not only autobiographical fragments, but a movie with a secret meaning and a rock-star couple whose daughter, Sophia, is thought by some to be the returned Savior. The novel wrestles with the first question that haunted Dick— "What is reality?"—and it suggests one good answer, based on a real incident in Dick's life. When a student asked him during a lecture for a simple definition of reality, he answered, "Reality is that which when you stop believing in it, it doesn't go away." Toward the end of the book Dick writes, "I lack Kevin's faith and Fat's madness. . . . I don't know what to think. Maybe I am not required to think anything, or to have faith, or to have madness; maybe all that I need to do—all that is asked of me— is to wait. To wait and to stay awake."

The second book of the trilogy, *The Divine Invasion* (1981), tells of an exiled or absent God—another Gnostic theme—trying to return to earth, which has been held captive by Belial, a fallen angel, since the fall of Masada. The novel involves a virgin birth, which perplexes the Catholic woman who is pregnant with a divine child. She says remotely, "Catholic doctrine, I never thought it would apply to me personally." The child must struggle to awaken to his own identity. As in classic Gnostic teaching, a perverse power holds the world in its grasp, and it is represented by both the established church (the Christian-Islamic Church) and the imperial political establishment, whose members are uncomfortably but profitably allied. *The Divine Invasion* is an amazing story of parallel realities, redemption, and the war between good and evil, with a wonderful ending.

The final novel in the trilogy, the last Dick completed, is *The Transmigration of Timothy Archer* (1982). The author based Bishop Timothy Archer on Episcopalian Bishop James Pike, who went on an odd pilgrimage into the Judean desert with too little preparation and died of exposure. So does Timothy Archer, in search of the truth about Gnostic scroll fragments. Archer is a complicated character: brilliant and selfish, genuinely insightful and clueless. The novel is narrated by Archer's daughter-in-law, Angel Archer. In Dick's novels, the point of view frequently shifts from person to person; but here Angel is the sole narrator, and her voice carries the novel, which contains serious arguments about Gnosticism and a few genuinely funny and politically incorrect jokes.

In these and his other stories, Dick creates characters who struggle not only for salvation, for ultimate truths, but sometimes merely to be decent human beings—and the two struggles are really one. What reality is and what it means to be authentically human are intrinsically linked. Dick's answers, such as they are, range randomly from new-age nonsense, through his own episodes of delusion and paranoia, to a Gnostic Christianity that contains more of the pain and compassion of real Christianity than most Gnostic visions. Many Gnostic writings advance an elitism that delights in being among the chosen in whom the divine light resides. Dick saw glimmers of the shattered divine light in many confused and struggling people, and he found something of cosmic significance there, both in the light and in the struggle. His finest novel, *The Divine Invasion*, for example, ends with the fall of Belial, the angelic dark force that held the good God at bay. Belial "lay broken everywhere, vast and lovely and destroyed. In pieces, like damaged light."

> "This is how he was once," Linda said. "Originally. Before he fell. This was his original shape. We called him the Moth. The Moth that fell slowly, over thousands of years, intersecting the earth, like a geometrical shape descending stage by stage until nothing remained of its shape."
>
> Herb Asher said, "He was very beautiful."
>
> "He was the morning star," Linda said. "The brightest star in the heavens. And now nothing remains of him but this. . . ."

"Will he ever be as he once was?" Herb Asher said.

"Perhaps," she said. "Perhaps we all may be." And then she sang for Herb Asher one of the Dowland songs. . . . The most tender, the most haunting song that she had adapted from John Dowland's lute books:

When the poor cripple by the pool did lie
Full many years in misery and pain,
No sooner he on Christ had set his eye,
But he was well, and comfort came again.

Philip K. Dick's fiction—perhaps because most of it was written in a genre known for conceptual risk-taking—dealt in an unembarrassed way with questions involving the ultimate meaning of our lives in a tone that was compassionate, often funny, and at some unexpected moments very moving.

May 4, 2007

Christo's Gates

*I*t may seem pointless, and in a lovely way it is, to install a
series of frames containing large hanging saffron rectan-
gles over twenty-three miles of Central Park pathways. But
after years of trying, in February [2005] the artists Christo and
Jeanne-Claude managed to bring it off. Called *The Gates*, the
project involved the installation of 7,532 frames, and the fabric
was hung so high that the tallest people could walk along the
paths easily. The money was raised by the artists, and much
of it went to pay those who installed the work, and to pay
monitors who directed people to interesting routes and also
used poles to unfurl banners tangled by the wind.

A gate is an entrance point, and in the Christo/Jeanne-
Claude installation one gate is the entrance to another, and
another, all leading eventually to divergent points—do you go
up this hill, down that one, or straight ahead? The light changes
as you walk, shining through some panels, shadowed in others,
and the winds change the vista. All is transitory, and by the
time you read this, *The Gates* will be gone.

What you notice entering Central Park (we started at the
south end, where the horse and carriage rides can be hired
and even on a cold winter day the scent of horse manure per-
fumes the air) is how many people are smiling. They are

uncommonly polite—maybe because so many are visitors and not New Yorkers—and a lot of them are taking pictures. I've never seen Central Park so crowded. The only negative note was a mad ranter who stood on one hill and shouted his message that everything about the world was lousy, but he may have been hired by the project to remind the international visitors that this is, after all, New York.

One of the most pleasant aspects of *The Gates* is that no one sponsored it. It really was free to the public, and not "brought to you by [fill in the corporation]." It sold nothing but the artists and their art. It was free to all, and given the quietly festive atmosphere, it plainly delighted most of the participants, all of those who walked beneath the bright hanging saffron.

It was also, I am sure, a delight to the owners of the Central Park Boathouse, which, according to a friend who frequents it, is often nearly empty in February. We went there for a drink and found it packed. We left the park by walking down the path where telescopes have been set up to follow the storied red-tailed hawks, Pale Male and Lola. They were expelled from their nest near the top of a tony Fifth Avenue co-op, but the outcry that followed led the co-op to construct a new nest. The hawks have in fact returned and are doing well.

Some of those who dislike *The Gates* object that it doesn't mean anything. Neither does good music, or good abstract art. But I have noticed—listening, for example, to John Cage— that his music can teach an acute and refreshed listening. When leaving the Museum of Modern Art after a couple of hours of the attention you have to bring to art, I have found myself seeing the colors and forms of the city outside with new eyes. It is this reawakening of the senses that makes many forms of art important, not any message. No good art is ever propaganda, even for the most noble cause.

The Gates reminded me of a Tibetan Buddhist tradition: monks construct a beautiful mandala in a frame with colored sands, an elaborate, intricately patterned work of art that symbolizes the fullness of the universe. When it is finished, the frame is taken to the edge of a river and the sands poured into the flowing water. The point is, in part, the passing nature of everything, as well as the fact that those things that pass are wonderful and can be sources of joy and enlightenment in the present. There is a Western echo in Yeats: "Man is in love and loves what vanishes, / What more is there to say?"

As far as I know, no Buddhist connection has been claimed [for *The Gates*] by the artists. A couple of people have pointed out the resemblance to paths at the Fushimi-Inari Shrine in Kyoto, where post and beam frames with colored saffron have been placed over paths. Christo and Jeanne-Claude say no lessons or points should be drawn from their always temporary works, and I know what they mean. But I think of the mandala, and *The Gates*, which likewise were there for awhile and then, deliberately, not there, and I'm grateful.

March 11, 2005

Not a Wasted Word

We all owe the people at New York Review of Books Classics a great debt of thanks. They have brought all of J. F. Powers back into print [*The Stories of J. F. Powers*; *Morte D'Urban*; *Wheat that Springeth Green*, 2000]. Powers (1917–99) wrote mainly (but not exclusively) about the Catholic clergy, and my uncle, a Catholic priest, was convinced that Powers must have had clerical spies who filled him in on what life was really like in rectories.

My uncle had reason to wonder about this. He was the pastor of the only Catholic church in Jacksonville, Illinois, Powers's hometown. His parish, Our Saviour's, was Powers's own when Powers was a boy, and my uncle's predecessor, Dean Francis Formaz, may well be the model for Monsignor Morez in *Morte D'Urban*. When Formaz died he left a will that deeded the church a sum of money for the construction of a new church building, but the money was available on one condition, one straight out of Powers: The church built with his money must be called "The Dean Formaz Church of Our Saviour."

My uncle could not abide the thought that a church built on his watch would give Formaz a higher billing than Jesus, and lawyers informed him that the will was iron-clad. So my uncle's solution—one Powers would like, I think—was to place the name of the church on the cornerstone of the new building, and he planted a small, dense forest of shrubs directly in front of it.

"Harvey Roche (later Father Urban) was born in that part of Illinois which more and more identifies itself with Abraham Lincoln but has its taproot in the South. Protestants were very sure of themselves there." So begins a chapter in *Morte D'Urban*, one of two novels Powers wrote, and he has my part of downstate Illinois dead right. That Protestant assurance was much stronger in the days of Powers's youth than it is now. Close to the time of his birth a pamphlet called "Hell at Midnight in Springfield" managed to combine anti-Catholicism, racism, and prohibitionism, warning citizens of the state capitol (thirty miles from Powers's home) against the evils of Romanism, liquor, and black men.

I mention this because a sense of the Catholic difference pervades Powers's writing, while at the same time his priests negotiate the same car dealerships, liquor stores, and furniture shops as their Midwestern Protestant neighbors. Powers wrote most of his best stories before Vatican II changed the face of the church, a change he was not particularly happy with, perhaps because that sense of Catholic difference was diluted. His stories, nevertheless, hold up; they work as well today as when they were first published.

Flannery O'Connor was a fan, though she qualified her praise: "Powers's stories can be divided into two kinds—those that deal with the Catholic clergy and those that don't," she wrote to Cecil Dawkins. "Those that deal with the clergy are as good as any stories being written by anybody; those that don't are not so good."

That's generally true, though there are exceptions (for example, the story "Look How the Fish Live," about a father, his children, and their compassion for a dying bird, among other things). His two novels, *Morte D'Urban* and *Wheat that Springeth Green*, are about priests. They are good, *Morte D'Urban* especially so, but Powers is at the top of his form in the stories.

Early in his career Powers won an O. Henry award for "The Valiant Woman," one of his best. Father Firman is saddled with Mrs. Stoner, the widow of a miner who is his nightmare of a housekeeper. Powers's description of their life together makes most bad marriages seem enviable:

> She hid his books, kept him from smoking, picked his friends (usually the pastors of her colleagues), bawled out people for calling after dark, had no humor except at cards, and then it was grim, very grim, and she sat hatchet-faced every morning at Mass. But she went to Mass, which was all that kept the church from being empty some mornings. She did annoying things all day long. She said annoying things into the night. She said she had given him the best years of her life. Had she? Perhaps—for the miner had her only a year.

He doesn't waste a word here, or anywhere. In "Prince of Darkness," Powers gives us Father Burner, a worldly priest, totally without a spiritual life, who resents the fact that his seminary classmates have all been made pastors, while he is moved as an assistant from parish to parish. At the story's start he is being courted by an insurance salesman: "'The Plan, Father,' Mr. Tracy lifted his seersucker trousers by the creases, crossed his two-toned shoes, and rolled warmly forward. 'Father . . .'

"Father Burner met his look briefly. He was wary of the fatherers. A backslider he could handle, it was the old story, but a red-hot believer, especially a talkative one, could be a devilish nuisance. This kind might be driven away only by prayer and fasting, and he was not adept at either."

Powers takes us through a day with this remarkably unsympathetic and self-absorbed man, to his meeting with the archbishop in the evening that will, he hopes, lead to his being named a pastor at last. It is a funny and chilling story, one of Powers's best.

It has been said that there is little about the spiritual life in Powers's stories, but that is true only if you are looking for something fairly heavy and obvious—a description of the experience of prayer, or something mystical. The conflict between what the church claims and the mundane settings in which it must make its claims can be found throughout. In one of his earliest and most moving stories, "Lions, Harts, and Leaping Does," Powers offers us the understanding of a dying Franciscan friar, and it is this vision that pervades all of Powers:

> He wanted nothing for himself at last. This may have been the first time he found his will amenable to the Divine. He had never been less himself and more the saint. Yet now, so close to sublimity, or perhaps only tempted to believe so (the Devil is most wily at the deathbed), he was beset by the grossest distractions. They were to be expected, he knew, as indelible in the order of things: the bingo game going on under the Cross for the seamless garment of the Son of Man: everywhere the sign of contradiction, and always. When would he cease to be surprised by it? Incidents repeated themselves, twined, parted, faded away, came back clear, and would not be prayed out of mind. He watched himself mounting the pulpit of a metropolitan church, heralded by the pastor as the renowned Franciscan friar sent by God in His goodness to preach this novena— like to say a little prayer to test the microphone, Father?— and later reading through the petitions to Our Blessed Mother, cynically tabulating the pleas for a Catholic boyfriend, drunkenness banished, the sale of real estate and coming furiously upon one: "that I'm not pregnant." And at the same church on Good Friday carrying the crucifix along the Communion rail for people to kiss, giving them

the indulgence, and afterwards in the sacristy wiping the
lipstick of the faithful from the image of Christ crucified.

Powers, more than any other writer I can think of, shows us
at the same time both the depth of sadness and the comedy
revealed by a belief in the Incarnation.

October 12, 2001

Philip Roth's Everyman

T he fifteenth-century morality play *Everyman* tells of a man confronted by death, deserted by friends, family, wealth, strength, beauty, his wits—finally only knowledge and good deeds accompany him to the end, after he has received the last sacraments. This is "a pilgrimage he must take which cannot be escaped." It is a grim and rather predictable tale, but the idea that it is true for all of us is at once obvious and scary; we want to avoid it.

Of course we can't, and some fine writers are there to make sure we don't. After I read Philip Roth's *Everyman* I re-read Tolstoy's *The Death of Ivan Ilyich*. Both are short and have a similar narrative structure: they begin with the funeral of the protagonist, which allows some vital (well, formerly vital) things about the deceased to be established before the business of his movement toward death is taken up. Then the story is seen from the protagonist's point of view, ending up where we knew it would all along. Both men suffer through their new and sharp awareness of mortality: they resent many of the living, often unreasonably, and find something terribly unfair about the fact of death itself. The difference in the endings is that Ivan Ilyich, who has been for all of his life only conventionally religious at best, finds release from fear and even from death itself in attempting forgiveness and reconciliation. There is no such release or hope for Roth's protagonist, who regards religion with loathing (as does Roth himself, something he made apparent in a recent NPR *Fresh Air* interview). "Religion was a lie that he had recognized early in life, and he found all religions offensive, considered their superstitious folderol meaningless, childish, couldn't stand the complete unadultness—the baby talk and the righteousness and the sheep, the avid believers. No hocus-pocus about death and God or obsolete fantasies of heaven for him."

Roth's Everyman—he is not given another name—is a thrice-married, thrice divorced father of three children. His two sons can't stand him, but the daughter loves him and is the delight of his life. He is deeply aware that he treated one of his ex-wives very badly. He has been a prisoner of his passions, a faithful friend, a devoted son and brother whose memories of childhood, the family jewelry store, and of the sea he loved and delighted in as a child all become increasingly important as he comes to understand that he will lose it all.

The specificity of what death means to each of us is there in both Tolstoy and Roth. One of the funniest and most affecting moments in Ivan Ilyich is Ivan's inability to accept that he really will die:

> The syllogism he had learnt from Kiezewetter's Logic: "Caius is a man, men are mortal, therefore Caius is mortal," had always seemed correct as applied to Caius, but certainly not as applied to himself. That Caius—man in the abstract—was mortal, was perfectly correct, but he was not Caius, not an abstract man, but a creature quite separate from all others. He had been little Vanya, with a mamma and a papa, with Mitya and Volodya, with the toys, a coachman and a nurse, afterwards with Katenka and with all the joys, griefs, and delights of childhood,

boyhood, and youth. What did Caius know of the smell of that striped leather ball Vanya had been so fond of? Had Caius kissed his mother's hand like that, and did the silk of her dress rustle so for Caius ?. . ." Caius really was mortal, and it was right for him to die, but for me, little Vanya, Ivan Ilyich, with all my thoughts and emotions, it's altogether a different matter. It cannot be that I ought to die. That would be too terrible." [Aylmer Maude translation.]

And in Roth:

But how could one voluntarily choose to leave our fullness for that endless nothing? How could he do it? Could he lie there calmly saying goodbye? . . . But leaving Nancy—I can't do it? The things that could happen to her on the way to school! . . . He saw himself racing in every direction at once through downtown Elizabeth's main intersection— the unsuccessful father, the envious brother, the duplicitous husband, the helpless son—and only blocks from his family's jewelry store crying out for the cast of kin upon whom he could not gain no matter how hard he pursued them. "Momma, Poppa, Howie, Phoebe, Nancy, Randy, Lonny—if only I'd known how to do it! Can't you hear me? I'm leaving! It's over and I'm leaving you all behind!" And those vanishing as fast from him as he from them turned just their heads to cry out in turn, and all too meaningfully, "Too late!"

Everyman is a dark book, as dark as it could be, with one medical setback following another until the end. Roth's protagonist finds himself hating a brother who has always loved him and has been good to him, simply because his older brother is robust, while he has suffered one physical calamity after another. In addition, the protagonist resents his sons, who still have not forgiven him for leaving their mother.

You wicked bastards! You silly fuckers! You condemning little shits! Would everything be different, he asked himself, if I'd been different or done things differently? Would it all be less lonely than it is now? Of course it would! But this is what I did! I am seventy-one. This is the man I have made. This is what I did to get here, and there's nothing more to be said.

He realizes finally that "he could not stand his brother in the primitive, instinctual way his sons could not stand him."

Roth can be as hard on his protagonist as his character has been on those around him. There is one long rant by the good ex-wife, condemning her former husband's lies and betrayals, and there is no doubt that she is right. And the sense that it all ends in extinction, that ultimately there is no meaning, would seem to make this a merciless, empty meditation, a long futile wail.

But it isn't. There are moments of remarkable tenderness in this book, gratitude for friendship and the love of parents and the beauty of the world, a sense that even if ultimately there is no divine purpose there are wonderful things and moments and people whose presence shines in such a way that we are right to mourn having to lose them. In one extended passage, the unfaithful husband goes to comfort his ex-wife after she suffers a stroke, and then talks with the widow of one friend and two old friends who are, in different ways, dying. There is a sad sweetness about these moments, as there is in a passage close to the end of the book where he visits the graves of his parents.

His mother had died at eighty, his father at ninety. Aloud he said to them, "I'm seventy-one. Your boy is seventy-one." "Good. You lived," his mother replied, and his father said, "Look back and atone for what you can atone for, and make the best of what you have left."

> He couldn't go. The tenderness was out of control. As
> was the longing for everyone to be living. And to have it
> all all over again.

Finally even fierce materialism gives way to the need for the
bones of his long-dead parents to speak. But this isn't, as some
reviewers have charged, simply sentimental, though it does
risk sentimentality. It is a deeply human reaction, and its
powerful claims on us are deeper than our expressions of belief
or unbelief. At a funeral, Roth's character says of a woman
whose sobbing irritates her husband that he can understand
her grief.

> It's because it is for her as it's been for me ever since I was
> a boy. It's because it is for her as it is for everyone. It's
> because life's most disturbing intensity is death. It's be-
> cause death is so unjust. It's because once one has tasted
> life, death does not even seem natural. I had thought—*se-
> cretly I was certain*—that life goes on and on.

Roth's character is not really everyman; neither, of course, is
the original Everyman, nor is Ivan Ilyich. Death happens not
to Everyman, or to Caius, or even to Ivan Ilyich or to Roth's
unnamed, baffled, sad man on his way to death; all of these
are imagined creations. But they are helpful reminders, like
the skull on the monk's desk. The medieval morality play is in
a way the crudest of the three, with labels pasted on the characters that are no more subtle than those old political cartoons
with a guy labeled John Q. Public facing, in this case, the Grim
Reaper. What is interesting is how alike Tolstoy and Roth are,
though worlds apart in their final view of death. Their descrip-
tions of the psychology of the dying are fascinating, and will
strike people who have been around a lot of dying people as
accurate enough. Just as Roth has been criticized by some

reviewers for being too sentimental in the end, others claim he paints too grim a picture of dying. Not everyone goes so uneasily or angrily toward death, they say; many have a faith that helps them, and many are medically much luckier than Roth's sad perennial heart patient. But many people, with and without faith, have difficult deaths, and face them uneasily. Roth's character may not be every man, but he is very much like many men and women, and Roth's book, like Tolstoy's novella, is in its way an act of compassion, moving and true.

July 14, 2006

Myths, Fables & Parables

*P*eople have been explaining themselves, their relationship to the gods, and what life means with myths for
thousands of years, before language began to be written
down and ever since. One of the first epics to be recorded, the
Babylonian tale of Gilgamesh, is about our desire to overcome
death. Norse mythology (my favorite) shows us that wisdom
comes at a terrible price: Odin, the father of the gods, plucks
his eye out and drops it into Mimir's well to become wise.

There is a depth in the Norse myths that I never found in
those of the Greeks, whose gods seem to be humans writ large
and stupid: bigger versions of ourselves and our passions. Even
if some of this is true of the Norse myths, there is more there:
the purity of Baldur, the trickery of Loki, who is so like the
tricksters Spider and Coyote in African and American Indian
traditions. These stories were easily remembered and passed
on in preliterate culture, and, when written down, became the
basis for everything literary that happened from then on, from
Homer to Joyce, for example, or Kafka, or anyone who turns
to fable and parable. In some ways the best modern narrative
work in short stories or novels functions as myth, offering us
ways to read and interpret our lives through Gatsby or the
brothers Karamazov.

Nonbelievers say that humans have created the gods, or God, in their own image, and that is certainly true of the gods who serve as patrons of wine, war, sex, wisdom, and so forth. Monotheism changed all that by making God essentially other, so Moses is not given God's name or any way to control or define him. "I will be what I will be." "My ways are not your ways." The Anglican theologian Charles Williams said that God commanded us to build altars so that he could send down the fire somewhere else. This is, I think, *essential* to Christianity. To think that we can know or conceptualize God in any way is folly. Any concept of God is an idol.

And yet there is something right in the storytelling element of our relationship to God. When I was a child I loved Padraic Colum's books. Colum was an Irish poet, playwright, and *Commonweal* contributor who wrote a series of books to introduce children to the great myths (and one for adults—*Orpheus: Myths of the World*). He was a wonderful storyteller whose book on the subject, *Storytelling, New and Old,* is worth any parent or teacher's time. His *The Children of Odin* was important to my early spiritual development, and may still be doing its work. I heard the gospel better for it, and I am sure that such deep listening can happen to whole cultures. A nonbeliever might say that this shows only that Christians, like the Greeks and the Romans and the Norse and Africans and American Indians, projected their notions into a fabulous realm and drew metaphysical and moral conclusions from fantasies.

Instead, I think that God made us as people who see our lives as stories with a beginning, a middle, an end, and a purpose. Myths address this aspect of our being. We need them at many levels (fairy tales are important, and children who never hear them are terribly deprived). God's revelation of God's relationship to us took storied forms, played out in myth

(Eden), mythical lives (the patriarchs), and history turned to mythic uses (the exodus from Egypt, the Babylonian captivity). The stories in the Bible—stories about Job, Ruth, and the prophets—form the way we think about our relationship to God. In Christ this is taken to a radical extreme: God becomes one of us, as powerless before evil as we are, and is murdered. This is not an incarnate god like Krishna, who can (quite wonderfully in the Bhagavad-Gita) switch instantly from flesh to divinity; Jesus was not a divine being clothed in flesh but a completely vulnerable human being who can be nailed to a cross and still be divine. This takes us to a new place.

In the story of the final judgment in Matthew 25 we see how unimportant ostensibly religious acts are, and how important unreflected-on kindness and compassion are (as well as unreflected-on hard-heartedness): in each case one asks, "When did we do—or fail to do—these things?" The lesson seems to be, this must become part of your instinctive nature, for good or ill. And there is the story of the two sons asked to work in the fields; one says he will, and does not, while the other says he will not, but relents and goes anyway, and is obviously the hero of the tale.

If nothing else proved the divinity of Christ and of Christian revelation to me, this would: Jesus tells the parable of the Pharisee and the tax collector, the story we most need to hear, in four sentences.

He knows us.

December 3, 2010

INCARNATION, DEATH, RESURRECTION, LOVE

Found, Not Made

One of the advantages of living in my Queens neighborhood is that on weekday mornings I get to watch little children heading toward their elementary school with their parents or grandparents. The school is a block from our apartment, and seeing all these children—most of them Asian in our neighborhood—lifts my heart. They seem happier than I ever was when I went to school, a place I hated, and in a departure from my usual mood I find myself beginning to understand why God loves us, and I get a sense of what it means to be made in God's image.

Sometimes what is obvious can strike us as new, and this is one of those times: everything comes to us through our humanity, through our participation in the human community—language, love, understanding (which is always communally shared). This blazes up when you see a child walking happily with his mother. If I were an atheist I would love this, but it is especially wonderful when you are part of a tradition that believes in a God who not only created humanity, but became one of us, to let us share his own being. This joins our being to all of creation, to glory everywhere, in the music of Bach and the rings of Saturn.

This sense of glory and the joy of creation can arise anywhere you look with the right kind of attention, whether close in—at fossils and shells—or far out—at nebulae, the Milky Way—and it speaks to what is deepest in us.

There are shells rimmed with what look like ur-alphabets, letter-like things that seem to move toward a meaning, almost as if they wanted to speak to us. They seem to mimic spelling, and that similarity can be seen as the start of a dialogue between the beauty of the naturally inarticulate, and the beauty and need for meaning and articulation that our minds generate and participate in.

We often reduce those moments—when our appreciation of beauty in nature or art moves us to joy—to the level of subjectivity, perhaps because such moments are so often fleeting. What is more likely true is that in such moments we are given a glimpse of reality without the usual veil of distraction and pettiness that obscures our perception most of the time. We are then, I think, closer to seeing the world as God sees it. There is something divine, for example, in Bach's music, and our delight in hearing it joins us to something real in the universe.

Richard Wilbur's poem, "A Wedding Toast" [*Collected Poems: 1943–2004*], has some lines that are not only lovely but theologically sound:

> Which is to say that what love sees is true;
> That the world's fullness is not made but found.
> Life hungers to abound
> And pour its plenty out for such as you.

This is what the Incarnation means, in one sense. We find it hard to believe that beauty is there for us, for our sakes, but it is. And we find it hard to respond as we should, because of our fallenness. In our response to God's generosity we too often project our own smallness onto God, instead of accepting the fact of God's generous love for us. We are surrounded by examples of that love, in beauty and even in our own hearts.

For example, when you see someone you love in physical pain or in some other form of distress, you wish you could take on the suffering yourself. Every parent, every husband and wife, every good friend knows that it is harder to watch someone you love suffer than it is to suffer yourself. And this should teach us something about the Incarnation. God has done this, the thing we wish we could do because of that in us which is like God, but can't do because we are not God. God became one of us to take on our suffering. It is hard for us to accept that kind of love, so some interpretations of the Cross have Jesus taking on the penalty richly deserved by all of us; but this posits a God who is willing to torment his son for justice's sake—a God made, I'm afraid, in our image.

The mystery of the Incarnation is not exhausted even by this, the mystery of the Cross. Perhaps those moments of joy we are graced with should be seen eschatologically—they are signs of what, finally, we are called to become, intimations of what the Resurrection will mean for us.

April 25, 2008

An Unimaginable Intimacy

One early morning not long ago, I woke with a strange physical sense of myself as the product of eons, rather than my usual tired twenty-first-century self. In the period between dream and waking I had the sense of being the son of a son of a son. . . . And you can go on way back, to a period where our ancestors slept in dens around fires in winter breathing bone dust—even to a period before language. That particular morning I knew that I was here now because of millennia during which human beings were formed by co-operation and cannibalism, compassion, and violence.

It is into *this* flesh that the Lord became incarnate, with all its mercies and horrors—a sign of complete and total compassion for what and who we are. The flesh assumed by Jesus is primordial and capable of so many wonders, and horrors.

The love shown in the Trinity and the Incarnation has to do not only with God's love for humanity but with God's love for all creation, for every atom of it. The love shown in the *kenosis*, the self-emptying of the Word become flesh (to combine Paul and John here), applies to all the universe. When we think of love, we think of what we can make of love as we have encountered it—paternal or fraternal love, the love of husband and wife, the self-sacrificing love of friends—but all this is not close, or is comparable only in a crude way, to "the love that moves the sun and the other stars," in Dante's wonderful words. We can only occasionally catch a glimpse of it in these other loves, and it is probably wiser to encounter our world with silence than to say, "There it is, that's what it's like." Love in whatever way we encounter it does offer us a clue, but a willingness to be silent before the mystery gets us closer.

The self-emptying love of *kenosis* happens in the Old and New Testaments, and outside of religion itself. It is in the burning bush, when God does not tell Moses his name; it is in the still small voice; it is in God's refusal to be our idea of "God," to step into the place we want our idol to be.

Kenosis is not only emptying but at the same time enfleshment (this is in Paul's text, Philippians 2:5-11), taking on our nature, being *not* "God," being flesh—which is to say mortal, passing, essentially empty, because death empties us completely, and being flesh puts us on that path.

The fullness of what Incarnation means is closed to us, and our minds are incapable of taking it all in. In Jesus an unknowable God (being unknowable is essential to what and who God is) is with us as brother, companion, fellow-sufferer, one who praises John the Baptist and tells a scribe he is close to the Kingdom, gives us saving stories, sits at the well with the Samaritan woman and even jokes with her . . . this is a shocking level of intimacy that ends in a shameful death, a death not at all noble by the standards of the ancient world.

I believe that this intimacy (and this upsetting of what we expect God and our salvation to be like) is so close to what it would take to bring our tragically wounded world close to God's love, and what it can mean in our lives, that it makes more sense to me than any other story, much more than the notion that, as beautiful as the cosmos is, it is finally without any meaning other than the awe it inspires.

But what Incarnation means goes so deep that our first stumbling interpretations are crude. Matter itself matters here, not just its fleshy human dimension, but any created thing. We identify with sentient beings, being sentient ourselves, and if we are Christians, we believe that God in his compassion in some way suffers with us all—but God is also in some way intimate with silicon, with gravity itself, with dark matter. Dante's love that moves the sun and the other stars is encountered in flesh; but how does it encounter water? It does, because water *is*.

In some way beyond our capacity to imagine it, what Jesus did on the Cross and in the Resurrection has to do with crystals and large gas planets. How do they come into the love and *kenosis* involved there? I have no clue, but that love and glory and God's own joy participate in being at every level is basic to our faith. When I say the name of Jesus in prayer I am not only naming the one named after Joshua who saved us on the Cross by his death and Resurrection, but a universal event that transforms a universe in which flesh and matter itself mean death into a universe aimed at transformation and life, in which flesh and all forms of matter reflect only God's love for all of creation, which is because he loves it.

August 12, 2011

Flesh Wounds

All the suffering we have seen recently—the dead Palestinian children, the casualties of civil war in Syria and the Congo, and the personal travails of so many—makes me think that what human beings must endure demands what the Incarnation offers.

This doctrine divides monotheists. For Jews and Muslims the idea that God himself became incarnate pollutes or drags down his divinity. For me, and for many other Christians, it would be intolerable if the God responsible for our being and, in some direct or indirect way, for our suffering were completely exempt from suffering, from how it feels to suffer what we do. If God is not tied into this life, if the particular suffering of humanity is not central to his own being, then something about creation itself is violated. One of the reasons Christianity and Buddhism stand out for me among religions is that both put suffering at the center.

The idea of incarnation would be scandalous enough even without the Cross. The idea that God takes on the fullness of creation, assuming it in mortal flesh, is shocking—and should be seen as shocking. But would a God who is not with us to this extent, a God who is distant from our suffering, be any less shocking?

The Incarnation is consistent with the confrontation between Job and God, and Job's willingness to question. Job is answered with what amounts to sarcasm—God is hard on a suffering man. That God even answers Job, however, is itself a kind of mercy: Why should God condescend to answer suffering humanity at all? The God of deism would not, we assume.

God's willingness to answer Job is the beginning of a mystery that deepens with the Incarnation. What is revealed in Christ is an identification so unexpected and, in its way, terrifying that we can't fathom it. It opens up a new way of thinking and speaking about God, one that begins with Paul and continues with later witnesses, Augustine being one of the most impressive. Too many people see the Gospels as prime witnesses and Paul as a later commentator. It's easy to see why, for narrative reasons, the compilers of the New Testament began with the Gospels and moved on to Paul, but in fact the earliest New Testament writing is Paul's first letter to the Thessalonians. All the Gospels were written after Paul's epistles.

What is astonishing is Paul's voice—new, I think, in the ancient world. I don't think you can find another voice this direct and confident, or another voice that claims an unmediated experience of God. I have long thought that the truth of Christianity comes down to the question of whether Paul was crazy or not. He made Christianity autobiographical, and he made its message urgent. Although resurrection was part of Jewish belief—one that separated the Pharisees and Sadducees, for example—it was peripheral to the Jews in a way it could not be for Christians, because of the Incarnation. As Christians, we have to see one another as people for whom Christ died, people joined to his life and death in baptism, people who, because of him, hope for resurrection, for he is the first-born of many brothers and sisters. As he showed in the parables, Jesus knows us, knows that we see our lives as stories, and so can understand the Pharisee and the tax collector, the prodigal son and merciful father.

More than knowing the flesh better than we could hope to know it ourselves, Jesus invites us to share divine life. The mystery of the Incarnation goes beyond us. Somehow it involves the whole universe: "We know the whole creation has been groaning in travail until now" (Romans 8:22). In Paul there is a sense I find nowhere else in Scripture of someone who has been gobsmacked by the discovery of who God is. He spent the rest of his life responding to that discovery.

There is much to celebrate in what unites monotheists. We believe in one God who is responsible for all that exists, who knows us and calls us to live good lives and to worship. Our belief in the Incarnation, however, separates us from other monotheists, and it is something we should rejoice in. We should not hold this belief in any triumphalistic way; that would be heading in exactly the wrong direction, because this is not something we brought about, nor something we can be said to possess or even comprehend. It is, rather, a joy we have been allowed to know.

December 21, 2012

What Is the Point
of Suffering?

I was at a wake for the mother of a parishioner when a boy, maybe ten or eleven, asked, "I have a question: If God loves us so much, why did he create death?" I answered—after an absolutely necessary long pause—that God wants us alive, alive in a way we cannot now imagine. That's what the resurrection means. But it was, as it usually is, a less-than-satisfactory response to the question behind his question. Once again you are faced with the problem of theodicy: Can God be all powerful and all good, and the world be the miserable place it obviously is?

A simple naturalistic answer to the most basic question about death is that if we didn't die on a more or less regular basis the world would get awfully crowded. But why is the movement toward death so full of suffering? Seen in merely evolutionary terms, nature gets us to the point of reproducing, and once we've done that job, abandons us to pain and dissolution.

This could lead us to adopt, or at least appreciate, a Gnostic point of view: we suffer precisely because some terrible thing in charge of the universe has made suffering a condition of being embodied. We are trapped here. Or we can take an atheistic stance: nothing is in charge, it is as bad as it looks, and nothing at the base of reality has anything to do with love for us, or with love at all.

We sense that we are meant for more than this, which may be only to say that we want very much to live, while it is equally clear that we are aimed at death. This feels unfair at a cosmic level. Why—if all works as it should work with the universe and what makes it run—why would we not be equipped with an emotional nature that went along with this inevitable decline, a way of gracefully losing it, nobly fading? We seem to be ill-equipped for our fate, designed to hate the thought of our dying. This built-in feeling that something is wrong is central to being human. We are not, somehow, what we sense we are meant to be.

Much philosophy and religion seeks to dissolve this as a problem by making suffering and death somehow all right. Christianity, to its credit, doesn't—until it falls into the hands of some of its preachers, who try to make everything understandable and even all right. Suffering is a punishment for our sins, or a test of faith, or any of the stupid things Job's comforters said it is. This great mystery at the center of our existence is not only not really addressed by explanation; it diminishes us to try to answer the question so simply, or even to try to think that we can have an answer.

If you could be that science-fiction creature, the empath, someone who could walk down the street and absorb the suffering of the people you passed, you would probably be destroyed within a couple of blocks—if you could get that far. I think of pastors, nurses, doctors, and other people whose work makes them take in great draughts of sorrow. There is a glut of suffering at every level: depression, physical illness, mental illness, resentment, the hard-heartedness and self-righteousness of people who refuse to be reconciled, poverty, war, torture inflicted by states, torment inflicted by families, bereavement. When you understand that suffering and sorrow are essential to an understanding of what it means to be human you begin to see something that only Buddhism and Christianity have appreciated. This is not an accidental part of being human. This is the bleeding heart of it. We are born, we suffer, and we die.

The reason this needs to be presented as news to so many of us is that in the affluent West it is quite possible to reach the age of thirty and never to have known death—a rare thing in most of human history. This real inevitability comes as a genuine shock. But the question remains, as it always has: Why are we put through this, if God loves us?

The important Christian contribution is to insist that God is not the author of evil, and that if death and the suffering that precede it have power in our world it is because of something else . . . sin is the usual culprit, and the free will of humans who are allowed to choose evil its usual means. There are problems with this answer . . . but one of the things we may begin to learn from what human suffering means (and they will not explain it away, or reconcile us to it) is, first of all, to see that it does have the value of showing us that the world, as it is, is not the world that God means us to inhabit. The second and more important lesson is that suffering and love in this world are inextricably tangled.

There is no greater suffering than watching the suffering of someone you love, or losing the company of someone you love. Every good marriage, every profound friendship, learns this at some cost. You are aware that one of you will die first, and the other will suffer the loss; and if one of you dies at the end of a long and draining illness, the other will have daily wished to assume the suffering of the other, if only it could be done. Any parent watching the suffering of a child knows the same feeling. And it is not only our children: when we watch the suffering of others, of other peoples' children, we are tied into their suffering, and in our best moments would suffer in their place. Paul moves us towards this understanding: "Why, one will hardly die for a righteous man—though for a good man one will even dare to die. But God shows his love for us in that while we were yet sinners Christ died for us" (Rom 5:7-8). Just as the love of a parent does not demand that the son or daughter be sinless—see the story of the prodigal son—so God's love for us is unimaginably generous, and is joined to the cross. This is a large part of whatever lesson the inescapable fact of suffering has to teach us.

August 11, 2006

Outrageous or Meaningless?

One argument against Christianity begins with suffering: a good and all-powerful God would never allow the suffering of the innocent. There is an understanding of goodness and of power here that should be challenged, but first it must be said that suffering has meaning in an argument against belief in God only if suffering has meaning at all. Its presence means nothing if one takes a thoroughly materialistic point of view. It has meaning that can be used in a moral argument against belief only if we know or sense that it should not exist. But from the point of view of a serious and consistent nonbeliever, suffering is simply there: we hurt, suffer loss and pain, have pain inflicted on us by others or by nature, and it has no deep, or even shallow, moral or ontological significance. On this view any sense that suffering and death are wrong, that they are violations of something important to our being, is simply mistaken.

If suffering exists and is wrong, something about the universe, intrinsic or extrinsic, makes it wrong. Some sort of deep presence or divinity is responsible, one that is malign or culpably indifferent. The sense that even some atheists have that our suffering is a wrong done to us is interesting. It seems to stem from anger at God for not existing, or for not exercising power as they believe a good God should exercise power.

I remember the late, odd comedian Brother Theodore—not a believer—whose prayer was, "God, if you exist, help me. And if you don't exist, help me anyway." The natural human impulse to question the suffering of an innocent child or the untimely death of a loved one is not found only among believers. We experience our suffering as outrageous: the world should not be this way.

This could be dismissed as a simple mistake, the childish reaction of an ego that believes its pleasure should be the center of the universe. Or it can be seen as an appropriate perception: the world is not now as it is meant to be.

The nonbeliever objects to the idea that the world is *meant* to be anything. For the believer the simple fact of existence points beyond itself, or to something deep in itself, something real that cannot be circumscribed or put into words. Wittgenstein wrote, "It is not how things are in the world that is mystical, but that it exists. . . . There are, indeed, things that cannot be put into words. They make themselves manifest. They are what is mystical." One could say that nonbelief is a kind of tone-deafness to this aspect of being and our consciousness of being.

That said, believers have to see that their own tendency in this argument is to move away from what cannot be put into words—away from mystery, from a presence that requires silence and silent witness—and to rely more upon dogmatic definition and moral declaration. We have a tendency to want to know more than we can know, and to be in possession of that knowledge. The great problem here is that "faith seeking understanding" can push us too far. It can obscure both the element of mystery—what simply cannot be known because in our present state we are incapable of such knowledge—and the fact that, for the Christian, faith is ultimately about our relationship to a person. This can't be reduced to a set of rules and propositions.

This is where revelation changes the way we encounter God. Moses is confronted with the bush that burns and is not consumed by the divine fire, and a God who says, "I will be what I will be." Jesus shows us the Father in his praise of John the Baptist, in his gentle joking with the woman at the well, in his compassion for the father who cries, "Lord, I believe—help my unbelief!" That the God who made the universe from nothing would praise one of us, joke with us, heal us in our doubting state—this is shattering and, from a certain point of view, ridiculous. How could the God who is present on all the moons of Saturn and in the heart of every black hole and the digestive track of every seahorse sing the praises of a troubler of Herod's peace in the ancient Middle East?

This is the scandal of Christianity. This is no way for a god—or God—to act. This good news is *too* good—it touches our suffering where we want it to be touched. We can see how someone might say that we are finding what we are looking for because it suits us to think that we are cared for, that God looks out for us as he does for all those sparrows.

But the one who reveals the Father suffers a terrible death, one that is shameful in its cultural context. The world hates and kills the one who loves the world. This really can't be called the message we wanted to hear, because we would avoid it completely if we could. We are drawn by this encounter into something different from what we would wish, and we are taken there with enough reason to hope, and at the same time to be afraid, like the myrrh-bearing women at the end of Mark's Gospel. We see that Jesus goes before us into Galilee, that this is our hope, and that in the long run none of what this means is up to us. Thank God.

June 6, 2008

Resurrection or Resignation?

Philip Larkin's poem "Aubade" is one of my favorites. It is a formally perfect composition, and its vision of death is chilling. The poem is bitter, dark, and thoroughly unsentimental in its view of death.

Larkin was not a believer (he considered religion a "moth-eaten" trick), nor was he the kind of blithe atheist who says there will be no "you" left to experience death or sorrow for not being. This precisely, he says,

> . . . is what we fear—no sight, no sound,
> No touch or taste or smell, nothing to think with,
> Nothing to love or link with,
> The anaesthetic from which none come round.

Like any serious Christian (this comparison would surprise him), Larkin finds death outrageous. We long for life, and know that we will die. He writes, "Most things may never happen: this one will." And he hates it.

"Aubade" may speak to me so strongly because of recent encounters with suffering and death and new life. As a couple of friends struggle to live with chronic, recurring cancer, another young woman gives birth. Two friends, about to marry relatively late in life, experience new depths of life as they are surprised and delighted by their love. Other people live with near constant pain, struggle with depression, work uphill against addictions.

We want to hold on to life, but much of what many of us experience as life is a very mixed bag, and it is impossible to imagine wanting to hold on to this particular kind of life for all eternity. Life as we know it is a limited, partial, wanting thing.

Christianity inverted the belief of the ancient world that this life is our most vivid time, and that those who have died are shadows of their former selves. In Judaism a belief in resurrection began to take hold, a vindication of Israel's just and a condemnation of the unjust; and in Christianity the belief that Jesus was the firstborn of those who would be resurrected placed resurrection at the center of belief. Paul insisted that life in the resurrected state will be so much more real than what we now experience as life that we are incapable of imagining it.

The best parts of the life we live now are hints of what we are called to. What we know is far from the fullness of what we are meant to know; it touches that fullness and makes us yearn for more than what this mortal life offers us. What we really yearn for can't be killed, or know death's destruction.

Of course this seems too good to be true, and believers must try to understand the skepticism of unbelievers sympathetically, because it does seem strange to think of everything we experience as a metaphor for something deeper and greater, to think of the life we live now as not yet our truest life. This can look like wishful thinking, and belief in God like a child's belief in an imaginary friend.

But the alternative is to believe that evolution has set us up for a kind of cosmic swindle: we love life, see something good in it, want to hold on to that good and experience it in all of what its depths seem to promise us; and at the same time we know that this can never be, that our desire to live will come to nothing, that this will be taken from us, often after a period of great suffering.

Those reductionist atheists who speak of their awe at the beauty of a meaningless universe apparently aren't aware of the near-gnostic implications of their vision: what lies at the base of a universe without purpose is that all of our most beautiful hopes and desires, the things that most define our humanity, are in the end meaningless.

There is a way of learning to live with this, but it means a certain hardening of the heart, a final indifference to things we are meant to love. Christianity finds death outrageous, as Larkin did. "Death is no different whined at than withstood," he wrote, and he was right. The doctrine of resurrection does not say that we can learn to accept and live with death. It says that in Christ what we perceive instinctively as evil in suffering and death has been destroyed, and that we are right to rejoice.

September 26, 2008

More than Sentiment

The word "love" is like some other important words (faith, trust, hope, care, wisdom, good, knowledge) in having a wide range of uses, extending from the most trivial areas of life to the most essential. You can trust that a certain toothpaste will do the job, and you can trust a friend. It isn't wise to park in a place where you might get a ticket, but this isn't what Plato meant by wisdom. A béarnaise sauce done in just the right way is good, and so is a saint. This broad territory with fuzzy edges, this plain across which a word can wander without being lost, is necessary. The point may be difficult to accept for those philosophers of language who really should have become accountants, who turn to philosophy and insist on a word meaning exactly one thing, or if not one thing, one list of things which can't move beyond boundaries with clear limits.

But a language is not a series of definitions so much as it is a series of gestures and a set of associations. A word like "love" is important precisely because it has such a multivalent use, and we would not be better off if the word could not encompass a love for chocolate and a love for one's children. In its roots in almost every language the word has to do with desire. In Spanish a word frequently translated as *love* really means *want* or *desire*, and although Greek has a theologically useful distinction between *eros* and *agape*, the ways we talk about love—whatever it means—vary so widely at times that we ought to look at them with some concern.

As Christians, we speak of God as love and say that those who abide in love abide in God. Here we obviously can't include every possible reach of the word, from the love someone talks about when he says he loves pizza to the love which is equivalent to lust, as in "love-goddess." To say that God is love and that we must love one another means something more than strong affection and attraction, even something more than commitment, as welcome as that idea is.

Christianity deals with incarnation—the Word made flesh—and with transfiguration—the flesh deified. That deification is shown to us in the revelation of the uncreated light of Mount Tabor and in the mysterious appearance of Christ as a stranger to Mary Magdalene in the garden after his Resurrection, and to the disciples on the road to Emmaus, and to those he served when he made breakfast for them and they did not dare to ask who he was. It seems to be essential in John's Gospel that Jesus appears as a stranger. God becomes human, takes on all the significance we ourselves give to what it means to be human. Jesus suffers, after being born into a family, as all of us are. He dies, and before his death his soul is "filled with dismay and dread." If we were to stop at this point with our consideration of what it means to be human we would already have a strong story.

But loving and living and dying take on new significance in Christ. Christianity found the word "love" and transformed it, found it as God found the flesh that was there, the kind we have, the kind God gave us. It is a word which is limited not only by what it can mean in theory but by how we, limited and dimmed ourselves by original sin, invariably do tend to mean it.

By showing us something we could not have seen without him, Christ has made the word "love" what it was not, and could not have been, without him. Love without Christ could not have meant "regard me as I regard you"—when that regard means a love willing to die for the other, an emptying even of the self, which under all previous definitions of love had to do with the pleasing of the self and the satisfaction of desire. A love which means the emptying of everything that can receive love is paradoxical—except where it exists in practice and can be seen to bear fruit in the flesh. So we return, through transfiguration, to the most radical incarnation.

The thing Christians must hear and learn before they can pretend to teach it is what love means, in the new light of the transfiguration of the ordinary language we use about love. This word may in its roots mean desire, but because of Christ it has been thrown into relief by a new light which shines behind it. If we do not understand the transformation of the word we use about our relationship to our wives, husbands, children, and friends and, most difficult of all, enemies, we will be likely to accept the culture's thin and sentimental use of the word "love," a use which makes its emotional component much too important.

The work of Christianity often seems to be to take a word or an idea and to turn it inside out. God so loved the world that he gave it his son, who was murdered for us, and whose love consisted in showing us at once an emptying and a transfiguration of the ordinary ways we think of love and self-satisfaction. There is what seems to be a deliberate upsetting of the categories we find important, and a joy beneath and behind all of it, in God's will for us. If we need a wide and sloppy use of words like "love" to be able to talk at all, we also need Christ's central and transforming example of love to keep our notions of love from being sentimental.

Our desire for God is part of what love means in this context, but God's desire for us is much more impressive, and unlimited, and it is a form of help which makes the word *help* seem very small. It is help we are given on our terms, and it brings us forward into places we cannot really imagine.

Think of what the Eucharist means: God gives us grain and grapes, and through our labors we make these into bread and wine, food we need and enjoy; we return it as thanks to God in the form of bread and wine, and receive it back as Christ's presence. This give and take is one in which God is able to give us not only what we need, but more than we could have imagined we could give or receive. God calls us forth from nothing, gives us the ability to work with him and take such basic and wonderful things as bread and wine from the surface of a world we are very lucky to live on. Our return of those blessings to him is given back to us as the Eucharist.

To have been called forth from nothing and given the fullness of divine life means that we are given life so fully, so completely, that there is literally nothing more we can do. We have only to accept it and try to live the consequences of what should be a radical gratitude. Despite everything we are given, moment to moment (Caussade uses the wonderful phrase, "the sacrament of the present moment"), we are cold-hearted, half-attentive at best, and bored. There really is no greater tragedy than our ability to be indifferent before what we have been given, and no better proof of original sin's real effect. It is a kind of fear.

June 20, 1986

A PRIEST
OF AND FOR
HIS TIMES

The Splendor
of Orthodox Spirituality

My wife and I visited Amsterdam a couple of years ago. Her time was taken up with business, and my days were spent exploring. There was a Catholic church close to our hotel and I wanted to see its interior. The church was unlocked on weekdays for the celebration of Mass during the lunch hour. The Mass itself was very short—no homily, only ten attendees, done in seventeen minutes. Used to much longer Orthodox services, I put this brevity down to a combination of the Catholic tradition of low Mass and the fact that Dutch is a very concise language.

Two things impressed me. Half the people at the Mass were young. It was a small group, but it was a weekday Mass and in its minor way contradicted the idea that the church is completely moribund in Europe. The other thing that impressed me was that the small gift shop at the rear of the church was stocked with Orthodox icons. The sort of religious art that many Catholics grew up with—bad imitations of Renaissance art, sentimental holy cards—was gone, replaced with icons. In some way, I thought, Catholics now find themselves reinforced in their faith through contact with images that were once quite unfamiliar to them, with a few exceptions (the icon of Our Lady of Perpetual Help, for example). How is it that the Eastern Church has, at least at the visual level and maybe in other ways, become a place to which Western Christians look for spiritual help?

Orthodox spirituality has interested many modern Catholic writers—Dorothy Day, Thomas Merton, and Henri Nouwen, to name a few. And while it is true that it is in many ways distinct from Catholic spirituality, too much can be made of this. I will go into some of its unique features, but it should also be noted that Western spirituality has had its own influence on Orthodoxy. One Orthodox classic, *Unseen Warfare*, is a reworking of *Spiritual Combat*, a classic of Catholic spirituality by Lorenzo Scupoli. Catholic theology had a powerful influence on Russian Orthodox catechesis from the seventeenth through the nineteenth centuries. This was in part a response to Protestant proselytizing, and even though the influence has been regretted by some modern Orthodox writers, who believe it introduced a foreign element of scholastic legalism, it can't be denied.

Orthodox are drawn to saints like Thérèse of Lisieux, Charles de Foucauld, Francis of Assisi, and Benedict Joseph Labre, just as Catholics have been drawn to such Orthodox saints as Seraphim of Sarov and, more recently, Mother Maria of Paris, who aided French Jews and died in a concentration camp. Her brilliant, challenging writings have been published by Orbis Books (*Mother Maria Skobtsova: Essential Writings*). The fact that for half our history East and West were in communion should make it clear that much unites us.

Still, there are some differences, which often have more to do with nuance than with substance. I like the words of one French Orthodox priest, who said that we should not speak of someone converting from Lutheranism or Catholicism to

Orthodoxy; it is more like adjusting a pair of binoculars. The same applies to looking at many of the differences between Orthodox and Catholic spirituality.

Orthodox Christians speak of "Holy Tradition," and see tradition not as an accumulation of habits but as the living language of the church, the received knowledge of what it means to pray, struggle, and understand within a community. Tradition is the way in which we are in touch with all those who have tried, in every age, to live in Christ. Although this is an individual effort in one sense—each of us has to be willing to take it up—it is also unavoidably communal. Before the recitation of the Creed we Orthodox say, "Let us love one another, that with one mind we may confess Father, Son, and Holy Spirit, one in essence and undivided." And a prayer before Communion reads, "When you desire to take the Body of the Lord, come forward in fear, lest you be burned, for it is a fire. And before you drink the Blood of God in Communion, first go, be reconciled with all who have grieved you. Then you may take courage to eat the mystical food."

The monasticism of the desert fathers is a major influence in Orthodoxy, and the *Apophthegmata Patrum*—the sayings of the fathers (and mothers) of the desert—range from remarkably practical advice to a startling sense of participation in the divine. Take these two selections, from Benedicta Ward's translation in *The Sayings of the Desert Fathers* (Cistercian Publications):

> Abba Pambo asked Abba Anthony, "What ought I to do?" and the old man said to him, "Do not trust in your own righteousness, do not worry about the past, but control your tongue and your stomach."

> Abba Lot went to see Abba Joseph and said to him, "Abba, as far as I can I say my little office, I fast a little, I pray and

meditate, I live in peace and as far as I can, I purify my thoughts. What else can I do?" Then the old man stood up and stretched his hands towards heaven. His fingers became like ten lamps of fire and he said to him, "If you will, you can become all flame."

Note the words, "the old man." The idea is preserved in the Greek word for "an elder"—*geron*—still used of wise monks and spiritual directors, the idea being that it takes time and patience to get there.

At the heart of the spiritual journey is the belief that we are all called to *theosis*, or deification. St. Athanasius wrote, "The Word became man so that man might become God." The boldness of this sounds blasphemous to some, but it squares with Jesus' words, "You are to be perfect, as your heavenly Father is perfect."

Christian mysticism is grounded in what is called apophatic theology, the belief that God's nature is so radically unknowable that ordinary language and concepts fail utterly to get at it—so it may even be said that God does not exist, as we ordinarily use the word "exist" to describe the being of an object among other objects. But God has made himself known, and by his gift we may share his being, as he shared ours. We are capable of receiving this gift because we have seen Christ's willingness to empty himself and assume our nature. As he became one of us, we can share the divine nature to the extent that with God's help we can empty ourselves.

Of course, this understanding is also found in Western Christianity. Both apophatic theology and *theosis* are present in the writings of John of the Cross and the anonymous author of *The Cloud of Unknowing*. *Theosis* can be found beautifully expressed in Gerard Manley Hopkins's "That Nature is a Heraclitean Fire and of the comfort of the Resurrection":

In a flash, at a trumpet crash,
I am all at once what Christ is, | since he was what I am, and
This Jack, joke, poor potsherd, | patch, matchwood, immortal
diamond,
Is immortal diamond.

But how do you get from here to there—from the practical advice to watch your tongue and your appetites, to becoming all fire? The discipline of Orthodoxy has to do with participation in the liturgical and sacramental life of the church, which includes fasting before the Eucharist and periods of seasonal fasting. More essentially, it involves private prayer, and this includes the Prayer of the Heart, or "Jesus Prayer."

The fathers of the desert practiced brief repeated prayers, often from the psalms: "God, come to my assistance; Lord, make haste to help me." The point was basic, to focus the mind on the presence of God. This gave way to prayers that incorporated the name of Jesus, and the most common form—"Lord Jesus Christ, have mercy on me"—is found in what has become a classic, *The Way of a Pilgrim* and *The Pilgrim Continues His Way* (HarperOne). Written by an anonymous Russian in the nineteenth century, it has what could be dubbed a "Call me Ishmael" beginning:

> By the grace of God I am a Christian man, by my actions
> a great sinner, and by calling a homeless wanderer of the
> humblest birth who roams from place to place. My worldly
> goods are a knapsack with some dried bread in it on my
> back, and in my breast-pocket a Bible. And that is all.

This prayer (which has variants—"Lord Jesus Christ, Son of God, have mercy on me, a sinner," and obviously goes back to *Kyrie eleison, Christe eleison*) is often accompanied by such aids as the use of a prayer rope, something like a rosary, and controlled breathing, to help with concentration; but it is important not to let the prayer degenerate into mere technique. The point is attention to prayer and the sense of God's presence, which means trying to arrive at stillness and interior silence.

The idea that one could experience *theosis* in this life was at the heart of what became known as the hesychast controversy, from the Greek *hesychia*, or "stillness." The anonymous author of *The Way of a Pilgrim* speaks of *The Philokalia*, a multivolume collection of writings on prayer, compiled in the eighteenth century. (The title means "love of the good.") The many contributors include St. John Cassian (c. 346–c. 435), St. Maximos the Confessor (c. 580–662), and St. Gregory Palamas (c. 1296–1359), whose response to a challenge to hesychasm in the fourteenth century synthesized Orthodox ideas about grace and our participation in the divine life.

Gregory Palamas defended the belief that one could genuinely experience the presence of God. Grace is not a created gift but the divine energies of God. Barlaam the Calabrian (1290–1348) had taken the idea of apophaticism to an extreme, and argued against those monks who believed that it was possible to experience "the uncreated light of Tabor," the light seen by Peter, James, and John at the Transfiguration. Gregory defended the monks, arguing that although God was in his nature unknowable, his energies were divine and could be shared with those who were capable of receiving them. Although it is possible to delude oneself, it is also possible to share in divinity, even in this life, just as Jesus shared our humanity.

It has to be said, however, that the point of prayer is not any particular experience, but rather turning one's life over into God's hands. One exercise that can help here is detailed in *The Philokalia* and is often called "guarding the heart." This is a form of mindfulness that, in effect, stands back and watches; it is an alertness, an awareness, that does not let itself be pulled around by emotions of attraction or repulsion. The first stirrings of any feeling—anger, self-righteousness (the two are obviously allied), lust, discouragement—are noticed, but the response is not a surrender to them, but a stillness. The word *apatheia* looks suspiciously like "apathy," but it means not allowing the emotions to dominate our relationship to God, or to others. Diadochos of Photiki (fifth century) writes of "the fires of *apatheia*." It has to do not with indifference, but with vigilance.

"The more closely attentive you are to your mind," says St. Hesychios the Priest (fifth century),

> the greater the longing with which you will pray to Jesus; and the more carelessly you examine your mind, the further you will separate yourself from him. Just as close attentiveness brilliantly illuminates the mind, so the lapse from watchfulness and from the sweet invocation of Jesus will darken it completely. All this happens naturally, not in any other way; and you will experience it if you test it out in practice. For there is no virtue—least of all this blessed light-generating activity—which cannot be learnt from experience. (See "On Watchfulness and Holiness," in *The Philokalia*, vol. 1.)

Hesychios says that "all this happens naturally" and can be learned from experience. The naturalness and experiential aspects of the life of prayer assume an intermingling of the divine and the human that is revealed in the Incarnation. All of us are called to realize this, and to the extent that we are made capable of doing so, it involves our cooperation with the one who emptied himself to bring us into the fullness of his own being. A prayer sung during the liturgy of the Feast of the Transfiguration says, "You were transformed on the Mount, O Christ God, / Revealing your glory to your disciples as far as they could bear it."

The idea that this glory draws us toward God is part of the vision of eternity of St. Gregory of Nyssa (c. 335–c. 395): "Every desire for the Beautiful which draws us on in this ascent is intensified by the soul's very progress toward it. And this is the real meaning of seeing God: never to have this desire satisfied." It is echoed in Pascal's "The Mystery of Jesus," a part of his *Pensées*: there Jesus says, "If you are seeking me, you have found me."

But all of this is encountered, as it is in Catholicism, in a complicated human context. All of us cope with institutions that have their corners of weakness and corruption, of self-satisfaction, and triumphalism. In reaction to these things, we can come close to despair. Prayer can bring us through all of this, but no account of Orthodoxy in our time would be complete without an understanding shared by all nontriumphalist Orthodox, and given its best expression in the words of Fr. Lev Gillet (1893–1980), a monk who moved from Catholicism to Orthodoxy, while insisting he had rejected nothing:

> O strange Orthodox Church, so poor and so weak, at the same time so traditional and yet so free, so archaic and yet so alive, so ritualistic and yet so personally mystical, church where the pearl of great price of the gospel is preciously preserved, sometimes beneath a layer of dust—church that has so often proved incapable of action, yet which knows, as does no other, how to sing the joy of Easter.

February 29, 2008

What a Priest Does

Recently I went through a period of deep frustration. I am a priest in a small but growing Orthodox church in New York, and small churches have all the advantages and disadvantages of family, or life in a small town. You are stuck with your relatives and neighbors, and with the members of your congregation. When it goes well it is wonderful: people can know and help one another, bearing one another's burdens; or they can pay attention only to the failings of others, seeing none of their own, and judge one another harshly. And everyone has a particular expectation of the priest who, if he tries to meet them all, will be doing something strange to himself and no doubt to the gospel. When you are caught in the middle of negative currents the dark side of all this can loom large, and make you wonder why you ever took this up in the first place.

I was in a dark mood one week recently, and it was compounded by a particularly busy and pointless burst of work: a lot of what a priest does in a small community is wait for people who don't show up on time, or at all, to do things like fix the boiler or wax the floor, and there are meetings, sometimes contentious, of the church board, and mailings to get out, on top of the usual pastoral work. The stuff that doesn't matter, or that involves you with confrontational members of the congregation, seems sometimes (it did at this time) to outweigh the things that do matter.

Then I visited a church member in the hospital, an old Albanian who only weeks before had been full of life. He's in his eighties and has Parkinson's disease, but always had plenty of energy and liked to preside in his corner of the church hall during the coffee hour. Suddenly he had difficulty eating, surgery was done, and it turned out he had a cancer that had metastasized nearly everywhere. On my first visit he was puzzled and unhappy, but could talk about what happened. On my second visit he had grown much more gaunt, except for his distended stomach, and he was quieter, resigned, but still able to talk about a young couple he had befriended. The husband had brought him pictures of their newborn baby, and he told me, "They're a very nice couple. She's a beautiful woman." He was still attentive to other people, but it was an effort. The last time I saw him he had gone into himself. When I touched him he opened his eyes and recognized me, but could only groan deeply. I told him what I was going to do, he nodded, and I anointed him and said the prayer for the departing of the soul.

The next day was Sunday, and the epistle was Colossians: "For you have died, and your life is hidden with Christ in God. When Christ your life appears, then you too will appear with him in glory" (3:3-4). The emphasis on the fact that baptism means our baptism into Christ's death, and the hope of his resurrection, is part of our faith. Seeing someone dying puts all of this on the line. It is hard to see the glory to come, though the cross is certainly apparent.

A lot of people visited as my parishioner approached the end. One woman noticed how uncomfortable he was because he was unshaven, and tried to get someone to deal with that. (She succeeded.) Other people fed him, gave him water to drink, tried in every way to serve him. Their attention to him, their concern, moved me deeply. None of them are blood relatives (unusual in our parish, where many people are related), but all thought of him as someone who was somehow in the family, and they were right.

I have seen this sort of thing before: people trying to get quarreling relatives to reconcile, for example, or someone wealthy who, without telling anyone, is of great help to a new immigrant family—I learned about his generosity from them, not from him. And in some confessions you see someone truly struggling to live the life we have in Christ. When I was in my teens, a Catholic priest told me that he found hearing confessions an encouraging and moving part of his priesthood. I couldn't imagine why, then, but I understand now.

Before a recent meeting of the clergy of the Orthodox Church in America a questionnaire was sent to priests. One interesting set of questions and answers had to do with how they felt about their work. Almost a third said they had regretted, at least at some point, the decision to become a priest. Almost half said that they had considered leaving parish ministry for some other form of ministry. But a majority said they had no regrets about becoming priests; 63 percent wanted to work as priests for as long as possible, and 60 percent of the retired clergy are still active at some level in pastoral work. Seventy-nine percent of the retired clergy "feel a sense of gratitude" for their work as priests.

That's a pretty healthy number. After my dark moment and an encounter with the more important level of what being part of a church community means, I see more of what it means to be a witness, and it is encouraging. You aren't necessarily witnessing, in the sense of revealing something, yourself, though one sense might lead to the other. You are, instead, able to watch grace at work in people's lives, and although that can and will take you to deeply sad places, it can also be deeply wonderful.

January 15, 1999

Priests Should Be Married

Years ago Austin Flannery, then editor of the Irish theological journal *Doctrine and Life*, asked me to write an article called "A Married Layman Looks at Celibacy." "We unmarried priests are always telling married laypeople about marriage," he said. "It's about time someone turned the tables."

In the same spirit, I want to say something as a married priest about clerical celibacy, and the alternative to it. At the age of forty—married, the father of two—I was received into the Orthodox Church. Six years later I entered the seminary, and was ordained a priest at forty-nine. I served as the pastor of a parish for ten years. I have observed both the celibate and the married priesthood. My uncle was a Catholic priest, and I talked with him frequently about his life. Like many Catholic boys, I considered becoming a priest. Having seen both approaches to priesthood, I can say that I believe the married parish priesthood is better from nearly every point of view, especially the pastoral one. But some caveats also have to be made.

First, something about the discipline. Priests in the Orthodox Church may be ordained after marriage; they may not marry once ordained to the diaconate or the priesthood. A priest or deacon whose wife has died must be laicized before remarrying. There is no stigma attached to laicization in such cases; a priest who marries after the death of his wife is free to stay as a lay member in the parish he formerly served, and is often deeply involved in its life.

There are sound pastoral reasons for these limits—or deadlines, as they may be seen to be. An unmarried priest who is free to court will have a relationship with every eligible unmarried woman in the parish that is quite unlike his relationship with other parishioners—not a good idea. In addition, this corresponds with the New Testament desire (see 1 Timothy 3 and Titus 1) that bishops ("overseers") or deacons be "the husband of one wife."

Bishops in the Orthodox Church are unmarried, and are drawn from the monastic ranks. From the seventh century on, the Orthodox appointed monks to be their bishops, because monks had a better record for being doctrinally orthodox than people whose fortunes were more tied to the world and the courts.

It has been suggested that the charism of celibacy will be lost in the Roman Church, or at least denigrated, if married men are ordained. Given a culture in which a phrase like "the charism of celibacy" is laughable to many, a culture in which virginity is seen as something to be lost as soon as possible, this is an eminently reasonable concern. Catholics tend to see this in terms of the Catholic/Protestant divide, and celibacy is certainly considered strange in many Protestant circles. In the Orthodox Church, as in Roman Catholicism, monasticism has been a central source of spiritual strength, and celibacy is essential to the monastic calling. Our bishops are all, technically, monks.

The operative word is "technically." Monasticism is at its base a lay vocation; in theory, monks are made priests only if a priest is needed to provide the sacraments for the community.

Many bishops, though, have little real monastic experience. They are unmarried and are professed as monks, but most have not had the long formation in the life of prayer that is the essence of monasticism. There are some sad examples of men who have remained celibate in the hope of becoming bishops, which is certainly far from the monastic ideal.

Nevertheless, it is powerfully inspiring to meet a bishop whose spirit is truly monastic—who has the "glorious liberty of the children of God" that should be exhibited by those who have taken it to heart. I have met three such bishops. I will not embarrass two of them by naming them here, but one is dead, and I will name him: the witness of Metropolitan Anthony Bloom is the reason I am Orthodox. The other two likewise conveyed the sense of what Irenaeus said, that "the glory of God is humanity, fully realized."

I am not sure that this power of genuinely charismatic celibacy can be communicated when celibacy is made a legal necessity for all priests. One of the bishops I mention above told a young man who wondered whether he should marry or become a monk: "If you don't understand that you would go crazy if you were anything other than a monk, it's not for you." It was a necessity for him, and I know he lives it well and consistently.

The healthiest celibates I met as a Catholic tended to come from communities of men or women who could bear one another's burdens; there, a generous and sometimes truly inspiring life was possible. But, although I knew many likewise inspiring parish priests, I also saw situations in which they had at best one or two close friends, usually other clerics, drank a lot, and avoided most other forms of human contact. It chilled me. When, as a young person, I thought of becoming a priest, I didn't consider the diocesan priesthood, which seemed isolated in all the most unhealthy ways, but the monastic orders. (I don't want to make it seem that this was a prolonged and agonized decision process. When I began dating the woman I would marry, I remember standing in a chapel and praying, "If you want me to be a monk, Lord, you have to make it really clear. . . . I don't seem to be heading in that direction.")

Encouraging and inspiring as truly charismatic celibacy can be, there are other necessary pastoral roles. It is helpful if a priest whose daily work involves him with married people and families is himself married and a father. Many parishioners have told me that they would find it difficult to go to confession to a priest who didn't know what it meant to have adolescent kids, or how to make up after an argument with a spouse. They wanted to know that I knew enough about "what it's like" for the discussion to go where it had to go. I must say here that I had Catholic confessors who were profoundly good listeners and very helpful in just about every area, and that this need for personal identification can be overstressed. But in fact the married priesthood does work better here, and discussions are more frank and practically helpful.

Although polls should not be taken as a way to run the church, it is interesting that while most polls show the majority of lay Catholics are open to the ordination of married people, I have not met one Orthodox who believes that the parish priesthood should be restricted to celibate males. There may be one, but he or she has not yet been located. That may say something about the pastoral implications of a married priesthood.

An argument that has been advanced in favor of priestly celibacy suggests that the person who is not committed to one woman or set of children is free to love all. This should be seen as nonsense. It should not be necessary to point out that if you cannot love one woman or child in the flesh, you can't love anyone, much less everyone. I do not mean at all that celibates cannot love deeply, but this argument won't do. Celibacy is a form of fasting from something good, not a freedom from the limitations of loving a particular person. And the associated argument from practicality—an unmarried priest can spend more time on ministry—has two sides. On the one hand, I have not in fact found celibate priests to be harder-working or more dedicated than the married Orthodox priests I know. Frankly, some celibates become adolescent in their approach to their schedules, regarding their time as their own, and resent interruptions in a way that most parents learn to drop after the first child or two. The other side of the question is the possibility that if a married priesthood increased the number of available priests, the celibate priests who are now stretched thin on the ground might not be burning out so frequently—though burnout is also a problem for Orthodox priests, for Protestant ministers, and for rabbis.

Now to some caveats. When celibates betray their vows, as Catholics have seen in excruciatingly painful detail, the whole church suffers. We Orthodox have not, so far, had a comparably painful trial. But when Orthodox priests who are bishops betray their vows of celibacy, or married priests are unfaithful, the church suffers. Just as some Catholic priests are men whose sexual problems led them to embrace celibacy in the hope that it would cure them, some Orthodox priests married too fast, in order to be ordained immediately after graduation from seminary, or ignored or suppressed the fact that their orientation was homosexual; some have remained celibate, hoping that that state would fix what they experienced as a disturbance. (This is quite different from the situation of a homosexual priest who is committed to the vow of celibacy.) When priestly marriages fall apart (or when the vow of monastic celibacy is betrayed), the whole community is wounded, and great damage is done within the married priests' families. This is not a frequent occurrence, but it is always painful, and leads to feelings of betrayal.

In the Americas there is another complication. (I can't speak of the Orthodox abroad.) Although the church is under the oversight of the bishop, who assigns priests, the church in practice is often congregational in governance. That is, a priest who might be assigned to a parish is interviewed by the parish council, which can tell the bishop it doesn't want him. This is not a bad thing, but in some parishes it leads to a mentality that sees the priest as a hireling of the parish. The priest's wife is often seen as an unpaid fellow hireling, and she is just as prone to being subjected to parishioners' judgment and criticism. While father-knows-best clericalism ought to be avoided, so should the congregational alternative.

One practical question is often brought up: Could the average Catholic parish afford a married priest, with his family's needs? It isn't easy, but it should be noted that most of the parishes in the Orthodox Church in America, my own jurisdiction, are relatively small—from one hundred to three hundred families—and that while most are not wealthy, they manage. For the most part, though, we do not have the parochial schools that many Catholic parishes maintain, and this makes a difference.

It should not be assumed that the priest shortage in the Roman Catholic Church would end if Catholicism were to accept married priests as the norm in the Roman rite. The Orthodox Church in America is currently able to staff its parishes, but within five to seven years, if the priests who are entitled to retire choose to do so, we will face a severe shortage. Salaries are not usually very high; one is unlikely to make more than a barely adequate salary. Most priests are able to feed and educate their children pretty well, but it isn't easy, and it frequently means that a wife is working and carrying her husband on her health-insurance policy. In a society which stresses affluence as a goal, few men are attracted to a life that means hard work and little material reward.

This isn't necessarily a bad thing. If the priesthood were a financially attractive proposition, it would draw hordes of people you wouldn't want to see working there. It has to be said, though, that even a married priesthood in our kind of culture does not attract a flood of candidates. Some people have noted the large number of convert priests who serve Orthodox parishes, and take it as a sign of health. It isn't. As a convert, I am happy to have discovered Orthodoxy. But I know that not many Orthodox parents encourage their sons to consider the priesthood.

Taking all of this into consideration, I remain convinced, having seen both arrangements, that a married parish priesthood is important, and a better idea than the alternative. At the same time, the celibacy that is central to the monastic witness should be encouraged and even celebrated in a society that has exalted sex—especially sex freed from parenthood and commitment—to nearly idolatrous levels. Still, monks, with the exception of the very few who can be healthy hermits, need monastic community. So do single men and women: not necessarily the community of the monastery, but more community than the church usually offers—a pastoral need that all Christian confessions need to address. Meanwhile, the blessed and sacramental community of marriage is the place in which most Christians find their way to salvation. The priests who minister to them should share it.

August 12, 2005

Gender & Religious Symbols

There are lots of reasons not to write about the ordination of women: it has been done to death, people have hardened opinions on both sides of the question, and you can lose friends (though no one loses a good friend over a subject like this) by taking a position either way. There are, however, some important issues the question touches, and they go beyond the question itself.

Neither the Orthodox Church, to which I belong, nor the Roman Catholic Church ordains women. The reasons advanced for this position often sound thin and unconvincing. The question for people in both of these very traditional churches is whether the ordination of women is a matter of church discipline, which could conceivably be changed (in Orthodoxy, a parallel would be the institution of a married episcopacy, or in Roman Catholicism, a married priesthood), or something deeper than that, something with almost the status of doctrine or dogma. A male priesthood is usually defended as if the latter were true. The defense points to the fact that Jesus was a male and, as important as women plainly were in the life of the earliest Christian communities, the priestly roles were confined to men, and have remained that way ever since.

This is met with the argument that Jesus was a Jew who died at the age of thirty-three, and therefore aging Gentiles can't play the part; another counter is that this makes gender too central to being Christlike, and consigns women to a second-class role within the church. Neither of these arguments should be dismissed as easily as they have been by some who oppose the ordination of women. On the other hand, both are, I think, insufficient. So is the argument that people who feel a strong call to ministry should, on that account, be ordained; and the flawed thinking here involves male as well as female ministry.

The argument that aging Gentiles cannot be priests is, of course, a light way to suggest that gender is overemphasized by defenders of a male priesthood. One implication is that the priest somehow stands in for Jesus, plays his part during the liturgy, and that this is the major reason for the male priesthood. That argument has in fact been advanced by some defenders of an exclusively male priesthood.

The idea of the priest as a kind of consecrated actor is theologically problematic; it is not the priest, but the Holy Spirit—the "least gendered" member of the Trinity—who transforms bread and wine. If it were only a superficial physical resemblance that made male priesthood a symbol that matters, the argument that an overweight Irishman of seventy is an inappropriate celebrant would hold water. If the only point of male priesthood involves genitalia—if that is all the symbol of maleness means—it is certainly a limited, and limiting, and oppressive thing.

Here an important question rises: Isn't it the job of Christianity to break through precisely those symbolic limitations? Only if they exist primarily as limitations, not as signs that might lead us somewhere. It could be that ours isn't the age to make lasting decisions in this area.

What about the charge that an exclusively male priesthood makes women second-class citizens in the church? First-class citizenship in the church is an obscene notion, and to the extent that priesthood is a form of status or power, no one should be ordained, male or female. For years too many priests expected a certain honor to be shown them; in recent years this has dimmed down into a kind of whine that asks only that priests be treated as "professionals," like doctors or lawyers. The existence of people like this is a much greater problem for the church than the question of whether or not women should be ordained.

What of those who believe that they have been "called" to the priesthood, and because of gender cannot answer the call? I expect that what I say here will irritate a lot of people on both sides of the question, but, as Martin Luther apparently did not say, "Here I stand, I can do no other."

Anyone who feels called to the priesthood, male or female, should examine himself or herself deeply, and go have a good long talk with a wise old monk (preferably one who has not been ordained) or nun. In the early church the "vocation" was a call from the local community or the bishop, and had nothing to do with any divine urging. The earliest monks resisted ordination as something that would interfere with their life of prayer, and were often chosen as priests and bishops against their will. Too many priests and ministers I have met have a need to be needed, a disease that can seem to those afflicted with it like a selfless desire to serve others. (One way to know it is a disease: they resent it when they are not, in fact, needed.) In any case, while the community does need to set some people aside to preside over the celebration of the sacraments, and they should be of good and generous character, the Christian vocation is one that comes with baptism, not holy orders.

I would suggest, very tentatively, that a male priesthood involves the same symbolism that is involved in the biblical view of God as Father; and this is not mere patriarchy—or maybe I should say that patriarchy is not mere, not simply a matter of politics and oppression, but involves symbols and resonances about which our age is tone-deaf, and which other ages have abused. The abuse of important signs and symbols is a symptom of the Fall, but it is not a reason to jettison them, in order to replace them with another culturally limited set of symbols that will then be abused in entirely new ways.

If the biblical language regarding God is merely a socially conditioned reflection of a patriarchal culture, then there is nothing particularly wrong with trying to change it. But if there is an important symbolic difference between calling God "Father" and calling God "Mother" or "Parent," it should at least be noted. The symbols are not simply interchangeable. Let me mention only a couple of differences that come to mind in calling God Father or Mother.

The metaphors surrounding God as Mother are those of fecundity—like the earth giving birth to manifold forms of life—and recurrence, cyclical return, and shared physical nature. God as Father is more difficult: a father does not have the same obvious biological continuity with a child, nor as clear a place in the child's early emotional universe. It could be that to speak of God as Mother is to speak of a God whose universe has no beginning or end, but is recurrent, a God whose relationship with creation is one of unbroken continuity, with creation something like heat rising from fire, or mist from a plain. It is not for nothing that we speak of Mother Earth. The belief in God as Father, however, may be more consistent with the belief that God created the universe from nothing, that the nature of God is radically other. The father is in some sense connected and at the same time an outsider. There is also the fact that in otherwise matriarchal societies, some priestly roles have been reserved to men. It is too easy to see this as a question of men trying to preserve power over women (especially in those matrilineal pueblo societies where a woman holds the primary property rights, and divorces her husband by putting his belongings outside the door). The symbolic nature of gender matters in ritual.

It will seem from the above that I oppose women's ordination. That isn't quite right. I do not believe it is the most important issue facing Christians. Nor do I deny that many Christian traditions have been based on, or at least profoundly affected by, oppressive cultural factors. I do not believe that an exclusively male priesthood is only a product of those factors, but it certainly has been affected by them. If a change comes about eventually, it should not come about, as it did in the Episcopal church, by a majority vote. Ancient tradition should not be dealt with so politically.

I do think the symbolism of gender is more than merely genital, and that our age is so tone-deaf to symbols of any sort, and so willing to put its faith in an essentially political interpretation of areas of understanding that do not necessarily yield their deepest treasures to that kind of forced entry, that ours is perhaps not the age to institute the change. Our work is to see that priesthood is a limited, if essential, service to the church; whether or not it is limited to men, it should never be seen as a form of power. To the extent that it is, it is un-Christian. To the extent that priests act as if the priesthood were a form of power, they should be forgiven.

November 18, 1988

When Church & State Marry

A t this moment in our culture, it is hard to talk about same-sex marriage without making a fool of oneself—hard to talk about it without appearing either to defend what looks like a form of bigotry or to endorse same-sex marriage as an unalloyed and obvious social advance. Both of these positions ignore so much.

For most of its history, marriage has been about the melding of families (it's still about this, as married couples often learn after the fact) and the protection of women and children, not, or not primarily, about romantic feelings. The easy dismissal of the definition of marriage as an institution necessarily involving both male and female—sometimes one male and many females or, much more rarely, vice-versa—is a problem. This has been a basic part of our understanding of marriage until so recently that the reaction against those who would dispense with it is understandable. But in some ways we Christians have, by acquiescing to the coercive nature of law, painted ourselves into this corner.

Until the ninth century Orthodoxy did not have a separate liturgy for marriage. People married according to the custom of their country. The empires, East and West, made the church responsible for the legality of marriage and its dissolution, and the distinction between marriage as a sacrament and as a legal contract was blurred. To this day we haven't gotten over this confusion. I find it ironic that a country that prides itself on the separation of church and state has made such a hash of this. If we were really serious about upholding that principle, we would arrange things so that couples—same-sex or heterosexual—who want a contract that affords certain legal privileges and comes with certain obligations would obtain a license for a civil union from a city or county clerk. Then, if they also wanted a sacramental union, a wedding, or some other religious bond, they would go to a priest, rabbi, minister, or imam. Some religious bodies would permit this, others wouldn't, but the distinction would be clear.

This seems to me a simple matter of justice. Anyone willing to make a lifelong commitment to another person should be allowed to. Such commitments can only strengthen our common social bonds, and in a society where so many kinds of personal bonds seem to be dissolving, anything that promotes fidelity should be encouraged.

At the same time, while such unions should provide the same legal benefits as marriage, they should also be seen as different from Christian marriage. But in America we have so confused the sacrament with the legal arrangement as it bears on insurance, hospital visitation, inheritance, etc., that the meaning of marriage as a Christian mystery has been lost in legalism.

This is partly because of the country's Protestant heritage, which never recognized marriage as a sacrament in the first place. But many Catholics—including Catholic bishops—have been guilty of the same confusion, though not all: apparently Pope Francis, as a bishop in Argentina, opposed same-sex marriage but suggested that the bishops accept civil unions as an alternative. The other bishops didn't agree.

It always struck me as odd that marriage is the only occasion when I, as a priest, have to deal with an agent of the state. An

Irish Dominican friend, trained in law, said, "I think the church should get out of the civil marriage business." So do I. My ideal—a sharp distinction between marriage and civil unions for both heterosexual and same-sex couples—might have worked if the church hadn't settled into such a cozy relationship with the state in the first place.

But the church long ago drank the Constantinian Kool-Aid in this and other matters, and continues to ask the state to enforce its own confused idea of what marriage entails. What we have to face now is not just a case of having lost the cultural battle over issues that matter—and should matter—to us morally.

We're also dealing with the church's ancient mistake of entering into an alliance with Caesar and asking the coercive power of the state to defend the church's morality. It seems to me a matter of justice to grant same-sex couples the same rights heterosexuals have under the law, and to require the same obligations. At the same time, to redefine marriage in terms of romance, personal feeling, and a rather Victorian sense of family, along with a sentimental approach to children, is a mistake. It is to act as if our present understanding of family, historically limited as it is, were the definitive one—the last stage in a long line of progressively more perceptive understandings of marriage rather than the contingent result of our current and, to my mind, overly sentimental presumptions.

There is and should be a radical difference between secular marriage as a legal contract and Christian marriage as a sacrament, a sign of the mystery that unites Christ and the church. If we care about the survival of Christian marriage, this difference should be our central concern. But we'll only get our priorities right when, as my Irish friend suggested, we get out of the civil-marriage business and wean ourselves from having the state enforce our way of life.

October 11, 2013

When Christians Kill

I opposed the war in Vietnam and was active in the antiwar movement. I would do it again. The war we are engaged in now [2002] is thoroughly different. Like many who opposed our involvement in Vietnam, I believe a military response was necessary after September 11.

Still, I can't buy into the just-war theory as it is usually presented; I have always found it impossible to accept as a Christian argument one which does not need at any point to mention Jesus Christ. The early church made people wait for years (sometimes even until their deathbeds) for re-admission to the Eucharist if they shed blood, even in self-defense. This was a witness to the gravity of what it means to kill even a killer—one for whom Christ also died. Participation in a necessary war means that we are involved in evil; but the evil may be necessary. We must go into this with a sense of mourning, an understanding that this is tragedy, and there can be no real triumph, only an attempt to keep even greater evil at bay. In Neil Young's song "Let's Roll," written after September 11, there are words which sum it up well: "I hope that we're forgiven / for what we've got to do."

Thinking about these things, I remembered the days when I worked as a draft counselor, and some of the military people

I got to know during that period. I found that I often liked them more than some of the antiwar people I knew. Years later my next door neighbor was a retired army colonel who had worked alone with some mountain people in Vietnam, seldom seeing other Westerners, and he loved it. His favorite reading during that period was *The Lord of the Rings* trilogy. We got to be friends. None of this is surprising—it is possible to be friends with people who are hawks, prochoice, or agnostic. It was a bit of a stretch, though, when I wound up regularly celebrating the Orthodox liturgy at West Point.

Saint Vladimir's Seminary supplied the priest for West Point, a reasonable drive from the campus, and I was assigned to go there. It seemed strange to me, though—the thought of a former antiwar activist celebrating the liturgy with tomorrow's military elite went against the grain; and besides, what about *my* plans? I had thought of remaining a permanent deacon, and looking for work in publishing. The decision to ordain me to the priesthood was made because they needed a priest for West Point. When I mentioned this to my wife Regina she said, "It should teach you that ordination isn't for you; it's for the church."

The drive to West Point was a beautiful one, as are the grounds once you get there. I liked the chaplains I met, and the cadets. There were approximately forty who described themselves as Orthodox; at most we had eight or nine on any given Sunday. (Like many college students away from home for the first time, Orthodox students used college as a holiday from churchgoing.) We met in a basement chapel, small and catacomb-like. The cadets were a diverse lot, from all economic backgrounds, polite and respectful to a fault, and serious about their studies. They reminded me of my neighbor.

Given the war our country is currently fighting, I find myself torn. I cannot accept the idea that pacifism is an appropriate response here, though Christian pacifism must be taken seriously and not waved away as if it were a merely sectarian quirk. My objection to a pacifist response here is that it will not stop the violence; our use of force seems right, in that it may lead to less violence over the long haul. But Christian pacifism is not about winning; it says that you might in fact wind up crucified, and that is better than killing, no matter what the cause. I can see a willingness to choose death for myself, but I cannot see passively accepting the deaths of people whose crime was showing up for work on September 11.

On the other hand, any deaths that result from our action—not only the civilians who die but even the terrorists—defile us. Our response must be repentant, and the idea of a victory parade is truly obscene.

What impresses me about many of the military people I know is that they often have a keener appreciation of the tragedy of war than civilians do, especially civilian political leaders, and this is probably to be expected. We might learn from that. At the same time, we must as Christians communicate the idea that even a war which seems necessary is tragic, and we involve ourselves in a mystery of evil. Just as Oedipus was defiled by sleeping with a woman he did not know was his mother, and by killing a man he did not know was his father, we participate in an evil, however necessary it may be, when we kill people for whom Christ died.

January 25, 2002

Why People Leave the Church

We have grown used to people who have problems with "organized religion" and "the institutional church," who say that they are spiritual but not religious, and who pick and choose from things as light as aromatherapy and the less demanding forms of meditation to cobble together a personal devotional observance. This sort of thing can seem fluffy and irritating. But some people who have moved away from churches and synagogues are more serious in their search, and their disenchantments are real and grounded. We should pay attention to them.

The scandals in the Catholic Church had to do with more than the sexual abuse of children and young men (and, less frequently, young women). They had to do primarily with bishops who seemed more concerned about the way this might reflect on the institution (if the truth were known) than about those whose lives had been blighted. One can see how someone might look at these cowardly people who are said to be successors of the apostles and decide that any truth worth living for might have to be sought, and found, elsewhere.

My own Orthodox Church has its share of scandals. One in my own jurisdiction has to do with the gross misuse of money, much of it collected for charitable purposes, by chancery of-